TRIATHLON
TRAINING BASICS

GALE BERNHARDT

A&C Black • London

Published in 2004 by
A&C Black Publishers Ltd
37 Soho Square, London W1D 3QZ
www.acblack.com

Published in the United States of America in 2004 by
VeloPress®
1830 North 55th Street
Boulder, Colorado 80301–2700 USA
303/440-0601 • Fax 303/444-6788 • E-mail velopress@7dogs.com

ISBN 0 7136 6993 4

A CIP catalogue record for this book is available from the British Library.

Note: Whilst every effort has been made to ensure that the content of this book is as
technically accurate and as sound as possible, neither the authors nor the publishers can
accept responsibility for any injury or loss sustained as a result of the use of this material.

A&C Black uses paper produced with elemental chlorine-free pulp, harvested from managed
sustainable forests.

Cover images © Imagestate

Cover design by James Watson
Interior design by Liz Jones

Printed in the United States of America.

Contents

Training Plans

Foreword

Triathlon has captured the imagination of many enthusiastic participants in its short yet illustrious history. It has become a way of life for
many people, young and old, and sooner or later they become fervent
students of the sport in their quest to find the ultimate way of being the
consummate triathlete. Mastering the art of fitting the training for three
very distinctive sports into a normal life schedule is a challenge in itself,
but perhaps herein lies our fascination with this great multisport event.

I, too, have been a student of this sport for many years and at the same
time have also tried to combine this with my passion for teaching and
coaching the sport. I came to the United States of America in 2001 to take
on the job of National Team Program Director for USA Triathlon. It was
only a matter of time before my path crossed with that of Gale Bernhardt.
It was through her involvement with the National Coaching Commission
that the two of us met, and I was immediately impressed with her pen-
chant for learning about the sport on all levels and her willingness to
impart her knowledge to coaches and athletes alike.

My regard for Gale Bernhardt over the years, as we have worked side by
side, has grown even greater. In her role as 2003 Pan American Games
Triathlon Team Coach, Gale established herself in my opinion as one of
the most astute coaches on the international circuit through her ability to
connect both with the team as a whole and with each and every individual

on the team. Gale has also recently been appointed as Olympic Triathlon Coach for the USA in Athens 2004.

Gale Bernhardt is someone who combines the mind of a scientist with practical experiences and insights of the athlete and coach, and she turns these pages into a thoroughly scientific yet practical approach to the training and preparation for an event. It is a practical one-stop guide for any athlete or coach.

Few people can capture the essence of triathlon across the wide spectrum of distances and abilities as Gale Bernhardt has done in her writings. She has presented her works in various mutisport publications and again here in *Triathlon Training Basics.* This is an invaluable resource for any person starting out in the sport, whether they intend to use triathlon as a means to enhance lifestyle or perhaps progress to the degree that they venture into the more competitive enclave.

Gale's unique ability to be able to address athletes across all levels sets her apart from any other coaches or writers in the sport. She manages to combine the science and the art of coaching this sport in an easy-to-read publication, making it a very important resource for prospective triathletes and coaches at any level. Whether you are a beginning triathlete or an aspiring Olympian, Gale Bernhardt's books can assist you in reaching your goals and potential and minimizing the risk of injury and burnout along the way.

Enjoy the journey.

Libby Burrell
Colorado Springs, Colorado USA
2000 Olympic Triathlon Coach (South Africa)
2004 Olympic Triathlon Team Leader (USA)

Preface

Triathlon Training Basics contains foundation information for new triathletes who are preparing for a sprint or Olympic distance triathlon. The idea for this book grew from the feedback I received from athletes who read *Training Plans for Multisport Athletes*. Beginning triathletes requested more information about standard race distances, equipment, proper strength training form, stretching, training plans with detailed information on each day of the planning chart, more guidance on main set swim workouts, and specific training plans designed for individuals competing on a team.

This book is intended to be a resource for individuals, clubs, city recreation centers, and schools in search of proven training techniques and training plans. Each plan within the book includes a specific goal, an athlete profile description, detailed workouts for each day, and suggestions on how to modify the plan to meet individual needs. Athletes with minimal fitness can utilize several of the plans in the book to improve their fitness progressively. Athletes who are fit and simply looking for a training plan to begin triathlon competition can use the book to progress from sprint racing to Olympic distance racing, then on to more advanced plans in *Training Plans for Multisport Athletes*.

Whether you are preparing for a specific race, creating your own one-person event, or simply using the plans to get into shape—beginning triathletes, this book is for you!

Acknowledgments

My friends and family are always top on the list of people that support my work. Without their words of encouragement, understanding when I hole-up for hours, and patience with my less-than-cheerful demeanor, I'm certain this book would not have been written.

Of all the chapters, the two that were the most difficult to write were Chapter 2 and Chapter 3. Chapter 2, the equipment chapter, was over-hauled more than any other chapter. Lennard Zinn proofread all of Chapter 2 and made excellent suggestions for improving the text. His technical knowledge is invaluable.

Award-winning photographer, Norm Rehme, did an outstanding job on the bike-fit, touring, and aero-riding images in Chapter 2; the strength training photos in Chapter 12; and stretching images in Chapter 13. He did most of the work for *The Female Cyclist: Gearing up a Level* and I was happy he agreed to shoot photographs for this book too. With his help, I didn't have to worry about the photography being any less than perfect.

Trent Schilousky and Kevin Hansen of Peloton Cycles are the handsome models in the bike fit photos. Trent (dressed in street clothes in the photos) has helped me with my cycling needs for years. Kevin (the cyclist in the photos) has helped me with a menu of cycling issues in recent months, including making me ride with him on an eyeball freezing morning.

Cathy Sloan is in Chapter 2, the model for the touring and aero riding positions. She is also featured in the strength training and stretching chapters.

Zapata Espinosa and Allison Clark, of TREK bicycles, provided the photographs to compare different bicycle models. My request for help came at a busy time for them and they pulled through for me.

Corey Hart from the Colorado State University Human Performance Laboratory did an great job of putting me through the paces of a lactate threshold test. In addition to his academic experience, his experience as a competitive cyclist and coach was helpful in the review of Chapter 3. Donavon Guyot of TrainingBible.com proofread Chapter 3 and provided a different view to improve the text.

Brian Quale and Lynn Peterson of the Colorado Acceleration Center provided the facility for the strength training and stretching photographs. Lynn was helpful in improving the technical descriptions in the strength training and stretching chapters. Lynn is the fit woman with long curly hair in some of the photographs in Chapters 12 and 13.

It took arm-twisting, but I was able to convince a few local fit athletes to demonstrate strength training and stretching techniques for the photographs in Chapters 12 and 13. Cathy Sloan is the woman with the straight hair and a black top. Nick Hansen is in the white tank top. Ed Shaw is wearing glasses and a white t-shirt. Donavon Haggas (balance board champion on photo night) is in the gray t-shirt. All of them are outstanding athletes, wonderful training buddies, and top-shelf people.

Brian Johnson publishes a daily web-journal, titled *Arete*. Many of the thoughtful quotes that begin each chapter came to me via his work.

Amy Rinehart of VeloPress supported the idea for this book—she is a strong supporter of my work and was patient though the challenging process of getting this book to press. I hope the process proves valuable and the book is a success.

Renee Jardine of VeloPress was the managing editor on this project, working with Marlene Blessing to fine tune the text. They can smooth my rough-draft text into smooth and readable paragraphs that flow for readers. Also, they made the editing process a piece of cake.

Finally, I want to thank all the athletes who have formed a one-on-one personal coaching relationship with me. Their trust and feedback has made prebuilt plans for other athletes possible. I also want to thank all the athletes who have trusted my opinion and prebuilt training plans to help them fruitfully meet their training and racing goals. Athletes often take the time to write and tell me about what a difference an organized training plan has made toward their personal success, and I'm not sure they know how much I value their feedback. I save every note. To know my work makes a difference is the reason why I keep writing.

Introduction

Although triathlon is a relatively new sport, its popularity is expanding every year. Training for triathlon offers the athlete variety—sidestepping the boredom that can creep into any single-sport routine. This same variety helps triathletes to achieve overall body fitness, cardiovascular endurance, and muscular strength. Chapter 1 provides a glimpse into the history of triathlon and outlines the most common race distances.

On the surface, the equipment needs for the sport seem simple. Swimming, riding a bicycle, and running require only a swimming suit, a bicycle in good working condition, and running shoes. However, if you open any catalog or surf any Web site offering equipment for multisport athletes, you will find an array of gear that can make your head spin. To help you make your choices, Chapter 2 covers equipment basics, including swimsuit selection, race clothing selection, and information on different bicycle models and proper bike fit. The chapter also covers basic shoe anatomy, gives information on heart rate monitors, and provides handy tips for training and racing. Comfortable clothing and equipment are critical for your longevity in sport.

Comfortable equipment is important. But getting in shape for a triathlon should be painful, because that is how the best progress is made. Triathlon training must be grueling day in and day out so that athletes can be in the best shape possible on race day. Right? Wrong!

These are common misunderstandings. Training at very high intensities every day can lead to injury and, at a minimum, burnout. To keep you healthy and making progress toward your goal, Chapter 3 provides information on how energy is produced and safe guidelines for exercise intensity. The Chapter 3 intensity guidelines are used in all the training plans, and all the plans vary exercise intensity along with planned rest to help you progress.

The first training plan in the book is designed for a person with minimal fitness looking to complete a sprint distance triathlon at the end of 12 weeks of training. This athlete needs a couple of days each week free of training. The Chapter 4 training plan begins with swim workouts of 50-yard repeats with rest intervals, building to a 500-yard steady swim. The long bike ride begins at a length of 45 minutes and builds to between 1.5 and 2 hours. The athlete using this plan is not currently running and begins the plan with five repeats of a 1-minute walk and 1-minute jog or run. By Week 10, the athlete will be running 30 minutes. At the end of 12 weeks of training, this new triathlete can complete about 500 yards of swimming, followed by about 15 miles of bicycle riding, then 3.1 miles of running in his or her first triathlon.

Chapter 5 is designed for a sprint distance racer. However, the athlete selecting this training plan begins with more fitness than the athlete in Chapter 4. This athlete may be going to a gym or regularly working out on his or her own program, which probably includes strength training. Swimming is a challenge for this athlete because he or she has not been swimming regularly prior to beginning the training plan. This athlete is capable of running for 10 to 15 minutes and is cycling twice per week. The cycling can be outdoors, on a trainer, or in a spin class. This training plan includes more training volume and more training time at higher intensities than the plan in Chapter 4, building the long run to approximately 40 minutes and the long bike ride to roughly 2 hours. At the end of 12 weeks of training, this athlete is ready to race in a sprint distance triathlon.

The training plan in Chapter 6 is designed for a person with minimal fitness who wants to participate in an Olympic distance triathlon. This training plan requires greater training volume than the sprint distance plans. Training time begins at 2 hours and 45 minutes in Week 1 and builds to about 7.5 hours in Week 10. The first swim workout begins with ten repeats of 50 yards and 20-second rest intervals between each swim. The plan builds swimming fitness to three repeats of 500 yards, or a 1,500-yard steady swim in Week 11. The long bike ride begins at 60 minutes in Week 1 and builds to between 3 and 3.5 hours in Week 10. The long weekend run begins at 20 minutes and builds to 60 minutes in Week 10. Fitness and endurance work is designed so the athlete can complete 0.9 mile of swimming, 24.8 miles of bicycle riding, and 6.2 miles of running (or run/walk combination) at the end of 12 weeks of training.

Athletes who complete the Chapter 6 training plan can move on to the training plan in Chapter 7. Also, athletes with good base fitness can begin training with the Chapter 7 plan. This fit athlete is capable of training and racing at higher intensities than the athlete in Chapter 6. Before beginning the training plan in Chapter 7, athletes can swim 100 yards without stopping and have the fitness to swim about 1,100 yards in a single workout. The athlete using this plan is riding a bicycle three times per week. Weekday rides are 30 to 60 minutes long, and he or she is already riding about 2 hours on one of the weekend days. This athlete is running twice per week, with one run at least 45 minutes in length. In addition to endurance training, this athlete wants to include strength training in the routine. Weekly training begins at around 6.25 hours in Week 1 and builds to 10 hours in Week 8. Due to this athlete's base fitness, training is reduced heading into race day in order to optimize performance.

The first four training plan chapters are designed for individual competitors aiming to complete a triathlon. The remaining four training plan chapters are designed for individual athletes racing on a team in a triathlon. These athletes do not need the endurance to complete the entire event and they are not having to juggle training in three sports, so their race fitness can be built in less time. They can begin training closer to the event and with less overall fitness than individual competitors, a big advantage for someone deciding to make a spur-of-the-moment race entry. All of the individual training plans for team members are 6 weeks long.

Chapter 8 training plans make triathlon team competition attainable by almost anyone. The swimmer in this chapter begins training by swimming twenty repeats of 25 yards, resting 20 seconds between each swim. In 5 weeks, this athlete can swim 500 yards nonstop and race with team members in Week 6. The cyclist training plan in this chapter begins with three workouts around 30 minutes long. The long ride increases to between 75 and 90 minutes in Week 5, and athletes are racing 15 miles at the end of Week 6. The first workout for the runner is 10 minutes of walking, followed by five repeats of running 1 minute and walking 1 minute. At the end of 6 weeks, this athlete is running or doing a combination of running and walking for 3.1 miles.

The training plans in Chapter 9 are for sprint distance racing and can be used following the completion of Chapter 8 plans. They can also be used by single-sport athletes with base fitness. The swimmer in this chapter begins training in Week 1 with a warm-up and a 500-yard time trial. The speed accomplished in this time trial is used as a base for building speed throughout the rest of the plan. The aim is to achieve a faster 500-yard performance on race day. The cyclist training plan assumes the athlete using the plan has good base fitness and the ability to complete two weekday rides in the 30- to 45-minute range, together with a weekend ride longer than an hour. Because this athlete has been riding consistently before beginning the training plan, faster riding intensities are included in this plan. Prior to beginning the plan, the runner using the plan in Chapter 9 is running 20 to 30 minutes twice per week, with a third run 30 to 45 minutes long. As with the cyclist, because this athlete has been running consistently before beginning the training plan, faster running intensities are included. Race day distances are the same as for Chapter 8: The swimmer completes 500 yards, the cyclist rides 15 miles, and the runner hoofs it for 3.1 miles.

The training plans in Chapter 10 and 11 are for Olympic distance racing. The swimmer completes 0.9 mile of swimming, the cyclist rides about 24.8 miles, and the runner completes 6.2 miles.

The Chapter 10 plans are for athletes with some base fitness, but without the endurance to complete longer distances. These plans can be used as a progression following the Chapter 8 or 9 plans. The swimmer begins with five or six repeats of 100 yards, following a 100- to 200-yard warm-up. The session ends with a 100-yard cooldown. Swimming endurance builds to a 2,000-yard workout at the end of Week 5. The cyclist is riding 30 to 45 minutes in one workout, 45 to 60 minutes in a second workout, and 45 to 60 minutes in a third workout. The first two workout times do not increase. But the third workout builds to a length of 1.5 hours. More hill work and some higher-intensity work is included in the long rides. The running plan displays workout details for an athlete looking to run/walk the event or someone wanting to run the entire distance. Week 1 workouts are each about 20, 24, and 20 minutes long. These workouts build to 20, 30, and 60 minutes long in Week 5.

Chapter 11 training plans can be used following the completion of the Chapter 10 plans, or fit single-sport athletes can begin with Chapter 11 plans to train for an Olympic distance event. The swimmer in Chapter 11 begins Week 1 training with a workout that includes a 300-yard warm-up, three repeats of 300 yards as a time trial, and a cooldown of 100 to 200 yards. This plan includes workouts that are based on the time trial performance, designed to improve swimming speed. Specific swim speed and intervals are in this plan.

The Chapter 11 cycling plan also includes speed work. Week 1 training has three key workouts, with two additional and optional workouts. Weekday rides are between 30 and 60 minutes long. Weekend rides begin in the 60- to 75-minute range and build to 2 hours. Due to the base fitness of this athlete, higher intensities are included in the plan.

The runner utilizing the plan in Chapter 11 has been running three times a week for quite some time prior to beginning the plan. Although running has been routine, running speed seldom varies. This runner is looking to pick up the pace. Week 1 begins with 20-, 30-, and 45-minute runs. The run workout time only increases to between 10 and 15 minutes per session, but intensity builds within the 6 weeks.

The single-sport training plans can be used by athletes looking to build fitness in one sport, or these plans can be used as preparation for training according to plans in Chapters 4 through 7. Whether gearing up for a race or just building fitness, athletes can either complete the single-sport plans in succession (one swim plan followed by another swim plan) or vary the sport plans (use a swim plan, then a cycling or running plan, back to a swim plan, etc.).

In addition to endurance training, strength training is an important component of fitness. Chapter 12 provides guidelines for a strength training program to complement triathlon endurance training. Many of the plans do not show strength training as a specific workout within the plan because the aerobic workouts that build endurance are the most important workouts for getting you comfortably through your first race. The strength training outline includes tips for good weightlifting form, common errors, and stretches to do between exercises. If you are not currently strength training, begin with the Anatomical Adaptation phase. Always separate strength training days by at least 48 hours.

The stretches suggested in Chapter 12 are detailed in Chapter 13. Stretching between weight training exercises is an opportunity to work on flexibility. In addition to stretching during strength training sessions, the program outlined in Chapter 13 is a good routine for overall flexibility. The recommended routine can be utilized after each aerobic workout session.

Chapter 14 is a very brief overview on nutrition basics for training and racing in endurance events between 1 and 3 hours. Hydration and fueling guidelines are provided in addition to formulas for calculating the daily caloric needs of an active triathlete.

General information chapters, such as Chapter 14, contain important information for all athletes. I suggest you read Chapters 1 through 3 and Chapters 12 through 14 before beginning any of the training plans.

No matter what your specific goals are, the training plans and supporting information in this book will help you achieve new levels of fitness without risking injury, boredom, or failure. The road to success is visible and waiting. All you have to do is follow the plan.

Chapter 1

Introduction to the Sport of Triathlon

I can't tell you the exact moment in time and space that the
sport of triathlon was conceived. Oh, for sure we'll discuss the common
theory of its creation, but the very raw and simple act of play, of athletics and
sport go as far back as you'd care to imagine.
—Scott Tinley, *Triathlon: A Personal History*

A Brief History

If you survey people who have completed a triathlon and ask them why they wanted to participate in the sport—what got them there—you may get an answer included in the list below:

I had too many running injuries and needed to do crosstraining to heal myself. Once I began cycling and swimming, I realized I enjoyed the variety and didn't want to stop.
I wanted a new challenge, a change from my regular activities.
It was a stake in the ground. I decided to make changes to my life and triathlon was the start.
I wanted a way to celebrate my next birthday.
I was decent at several sports and the idea of combining them into a single competition seemed to be to my advantage.

I watched a multisport event and thought the madness looked like great fun.

It's a great way to stay fit because I get an overall workout—cycling and running do nothing for my upper body.

My buddies and I made a bet. I say a good cyclist can slaughter a good runner or a good swimmer in a multisport event. My buddies disagree. I guess we'll just have to test those theories. Bring on the race.

Some of the comments listed above were among the reasons for the first triathlon staged in the United States. Dave Pain's birthday celebration, "Dave Pain's Birthday Biathlon," was one of the seeds for the sport of triathlon as we know it today—swimming, cycling, and running. Dave organized a run/swim event to celebrate his fiftieth birthday by inviting a few of his buddies to run 4.2 miles around Fiesta Island near San Diego, then swim across the estuary just south of the Hilton Hotel. Dave selected swimming and running because he was a decent swimmer and back in 1972 "everybody ran."

A few years later, Jack Johnstone and Don Shanahan both had ideas to enhance the run/swim events that were already popular in the San Diego area. Jack wanted to stage an event with multiple running and swimming legs within a single event, an idea that evolved from Dave Pain's Birthday Biathlon. Don Shanahan was aware of the many biathlons in the area that were mostly lifeguard competitions, but had no knowledge of Pain's biathlon. Don was also on the board of the San Diego Track Club. An avid athlete himself, his running would occasionally sideline him with injuries, so he took up cycling. From his cycling, he realized it would be a good idea to add cycling at the end of one of the biathlons and made that suggestion to the track club board. Although the board wasn't necessarily thrilled with the idea, another board member, Dave Pain, suggested that Don contact Jack.

Together Jack and Don organized the Mission Bay Triathlon in 1974. The San Diego Track Club announced its new event in the club newsletter: "Run, Cycle, Swim—Triathlon set for the 25th." This appears to be the first time that the word "triathlon" was used in the modern sense. There was an event in the 1904 Olympic Games called "triathlon," consisting of the long jump, shot put, and 100-yard dash. On September 4, 1921, an event titled *"Course des Trois Sports"* (race of three sports) was held at the Petit Pavillon Swim Club in Marseille, France. Lulu Telmat, the woman who won the race, cycled, ran, and swam her way to victory.

In the early triathlons, it was common to place swimming as the last event. It seemed logical to swim at the end of the race in order to cool off. As more competitors enjoyed the experience of a triathlon, it became obvious it was unsafe to swim at the end of the event. People experienced cramps and developed fatigue during the swim, making for dangerous conditions. Today, most triathlons are staged in a swim–bike–run sequence, although a few exceptions remain.

While this book is written for beginner triathletes, it seems appropriate to mention the Ironman® Triathlon. Undeniably, the press coverage of the Ironman® Triathlon launched triathlon into public view, both intriguing and inviting viewers from all walks of life to challenge themselves by participating in a triathlon. Just where did the wacky idea to swim 2.4 miles, bike 112 miles, and run 26.2 miles come from? John Collins.

John, a U.S. Naval officer, was one of the participants in the first Mission Bay Triathlon. In 1977, at the awards ceremony for the Oahu Perimeter running relay race, he challenged those in attendance to compete in the first ironman triathlon, which combined three of Oahu's endurance events into a single event. He combined the Waikiki Rough Water Swim, the Around-Oahu Bike Ride, and the Honolulu Marathon into one race. On February 18, 1978, only fifteen men lined up at the start of the race and twelve of them finished. Gordon Haller crossed the finish line first, with a time of 11:46.58.

In the United States, the triathlon's popularity grew in the 1980s. The sport's first national publication, *Triathlete* magazine, was born in 1982, as well as the U.S. Triathlon Association (later U.S. Triathlon Federation and then U.S.A. Triathlon), its first governing body. In 1989, an international governing body was formed, International Triathlon Union (ITU), whose focus was to gain acceptance by the International Olympic Committee and have triathlon added to the Olympic program. Triathlon was named to the Olympic program in 1994 and debuted as an Olympic medal sport at the 2000 Olympic Games in Sydney, Australia. The

Olympic triathlon distances are for a 1.5-kilometer swim, 40-kilometer bike ride, and 10-kilometer run.

Common Race Distances

There are four common race distances for triathlon competitions. However, sometimes location dictates distance. Race directors may be challenged to find a safe venue for a swim–bike–run event. To keep the logistics and safety concerns of staging such an event to a dull roar, on occasion race directors wisely select a racecourse that differs slightly from the common distances mentioned here. Thankfully, good race directors and benevolent volunteers continue to host these events at a growing number of locations, some of which are world-class. Often race directors provide not only individual competitor categories but team categories as well. For many single-sport athletes, team competition adds a new camaraderie to their solo training.

Sprint Distance

A sprint distance triathlon is often the best way for new triathletes to have a positive experience in their first event. A typical sprint distance event consists of 400 to 500 yards (or meters) of swimming, 12 to 15 miles of cycling, and a run of 3.1 miles. These distances make completing the event quite manageable for fit and soon-to-be-fit athletes.

Olympic Distance

In the late 1980s, a 1.5-kilometer swim, 40-kilometer bike ride, and 10-kilometer run (0.9 mile swimming, 24.8-mile bike ride, and 6.2-mile run) was often called "International Distance Triathlon" because that distance was accepted as the international standard and used at the first Triathlon World Championship. That championship was held August 6, 1989, in Avignon, France, and the winners were Erin Baker of New Zealand and Mark Allen of the United States.

In 1994 the International Triathlon Union (ITU), led by president Les McDonald, convinced the International Olympic Committee to make triathlon an Olympic sport for the Sydney Games of 2000. Prior to 2000, triathlon was not a sport represented at the Olympics. The process for elite athletes to qualify and race in the Olympics requires the accumulation of ITU points acquired at ITU-sanctioned races. Currently, triathletes must be ranked in the top 125 in the world to be eligible to compete in the Olympic Games. The process for Olympic qualification varies for each country.

At the Olympics, as well as elite-level ITU racing, triathlon is draft-legal. This means athletes can ride in very close formation during the bicycle portion of the event. Riding close behind another rider or in a group of riders is a great advantage, saving the drafting cyclists as much as 30 percent of their energy expenditure. As you can imagine, saving energy can add up to a big advantage.

The focus of this book is on the non-drafting race format. Complete rules for non-drafting races can be found at http://www.usatriathlon.org. As of the writing of this book, draft-legal racing is limited to elite athletes racing at ITU events and seeking points to qualify for eligibility to compete at the Olympic Games.

Half-Ironman Distance

For athletes wanting to increase their endurance without leaping to an ironman-distance event, a half-ironman event is perfect. These events are typically 1.2 miles of swimming, 56 miles of cycling, and 13.1 miles of running.

Ironman Distance

The original distances for an ironman race, established by John Collins, remain the standard for ironman racing today: a 2.4-mile swim, followed by a 112-mile bike ride, topped off with a 26.2-mile run. Once bitten by the ironman bug, many athletes spend countless hours scheming and dreaming of "a faster race." For others, simply completing this distance once in a lifetime is plenty.

More Thoughts

I completed my first triathlon in 1987. When I began research for this book, I noticed much of the history of the sport dates to the 1970s and 1980s. *Hey, wait a minute! I'm not that old!* And neither is the sport of triathlon, compared with the individual sports of swimming, cycling, and running. Luckily, many of the legends of the sport of triathlon are still living. Many of their names appear in the text, and photographs of them can be seen in the book *Triathlon: A Personal History* by Scott Tinley.

References

Johnstone, Jack. "Triathlon: The Early History of the Sport," http://home. san.rr.com/johnstone.

Tinley, Scott. *Triathlon: A Personal History.* Boulder, CO: VeloPress, 1998.

Triathlon International Marseille, History, http://www.triathlon-marseille. com/historique.html.

USA Triathlon, "History of Triathlon." http://www.usatriathlon.org/ viewRelease.asp?File=01-11-1999_3.txt.

USA Triathlon, "History of Triathlon Timeline." http://www.usatriathlon. org/viewRelease.asp?File=02-11-1999_1.txt.

USA Triathlon, "USA Triathlon History." http://www.usatriathlon.org/ viewRelease.asp?File=01-11-1999_0.txt.

Chapter 2

Equipment

*After these years of experience, I look with amazement on our
audacity in attempting flights with a new and untried machine
under such circumstances.*
—Orville Wright (1871–1948)

In most triathlons, swimming is the first event, followed by cycling, then running. Your overall time in the event is the total time it takes you to swim, travel from the water to your bike and transition to cycling gear, ride the course, change from cycling to running gear, and complete the event with a run. The first transition, from swimming to cycling, is often called "T1." The second transition, from cycling to running, is often called "T2." The event really comprises the three primary sports of swimming, cycling, and running, plus the transitions.

For most beginners, the main goal for the first triathlon is to "finish with a smile on my face." To some, this phrase means getting across the finish line with minimal discomfort; while for others, it means crossing the finish line in the least amount of time or aiming for a fast time. Those in the first category are looking to complete the race, and those in the second category are looking to compete. Sometimes, the equipment chosen by athletes looking to complete the event is different from that chosen by athletes looking to compete.

In the simplest form, the only equipment needed for participating in a triathlon are a swimsuit, a bicycle, and a good pair of running shoes. These items are readily available to most people—even if a borrowed bicycle is your trusty steed. Some athletes prefer this simplicity, while others are attracted to the multitude of gadgets available to multisport athletes. This chapter covers basic information on equipment for triathlon training and racing.

Swim

For swim training and racing, it is possible to complete your first event with only a swimsuit and a pair of goggles. Once you begin looking around, you will find there is a wide selection of swimsuit styles, goggles, the option of a wet suit for open-water swimming, and a variety of swimming pool toys.

Swimsuits

There are many different styles of swimsuits available on the market. You may decide to train in a different style of suit than you use for racing. For training, many athletes select suits made of polyester, nylon, or a blend, because they tend to stand up well to chlorine. Racing suits are typically made from Lycra™ spandex or similar specialty materials. They are tight-fitting and more stretchy-feeling than the polyester or nylon suits. The snugness allows for a more hydrodynamic fit and less drag to slow you down.

Wear a Swimsuit for the Entire Race?

To choose your outfit for race day, you should consider the following questions:

Are you comfortable? If you select a swimsuit to race in, it is important that the leg elastic be neither too tight nor too loose. Either extreme will make you uncomfortable during the race. For women, the top straps of the suit need to be comfortable and not cut into shoulders or armpit areas.

Does the suit style or fit offer ample coverage? For the guys, one athlete will find comfort in a tight-fitting racer's-cut suit; while someone else will be more comfortable in a trunk-style suit that has longer legs and more coverage. For the gals, a sunbathing suit is seldom comfortable for training and racing.

Do you plan to wear the clothing you swim in for the entire race? Many athletes, male and female, choose to complete the entire race in a swimsuit. Other athletes prefer another option:

At races that include a pool swim, often the run from the pool to the transition area is routed through the locker room. Athletes can change from a swimsuit to cycling attire in the locker room. Know that trying to get into cycling gear when your body is damp is quite a challenge. This changing time adds to your overall race time.

Some athletes feel more comfortable slipping a pair of running shorts over their swimsuits to give added coverage. Be aware that the inner leg seams on running shorts may rub between your leg and the bike seat with each pedal stroke, chafing you.

Instead of a traditional swimsuit, some athletes use a suit specifically designed for multisport activities. Some of these special suits are designed exactly like a swimsuit, except that they have extra padding in the crotch area to add comfort for the cycling portion of the event. Other designs include a tank top with shorts that look like cycling shorts. However, the length of the inseam is shorter and the crotch padding is lighter than on traditional cycling shorts. A third choice is a skin suit, or a one-piece suit. The top of a skin suit has short sleeves like a cycling jersey or it is sleeveless. The shorts are either traditional cycling length or the cropped variety. Entry into the suit is through a zipper that runs down the front of your body.

Quick Tip Use waterproof athletic tape to secure the end of your watch strap on race day.

Wet Suits

Some sprint races and Olympic distance races are in open-water situations. A wet suit can provide additional warmth and buoyancy. These factors translate to more comfort, energy conservation, and speed. Races that are sanctioned by USA Triathlon allow wet suits for age group athletes when the water temperature is below 74 degrees Fahrenheit. (Complete rules can be found at the USA Triathlon Web site at http://www. usatriathlon.org.)

Are sleeveless wet suits better than full-sleeved suits? The answer to this question depends on personal preference and comfort. Athletes racing in colder water conditions often prefer full-sleeved suits. Those racing in warmer conditions or athletes with wide shoulders often prefer sleeveless suits. Sleeveless suits keep athletes cooler while still providing buoyancy. Triathletes with wide or muscular shoulders and arms prefer sleeveless suits because they feel less restricted and have a better range of motion for swimming.

Just because a race is in open water does not mean you must wear a wet suit. The only time a wet suit is a must is in cold water. Many beginning racers prefer to race without a wet suit until they fall in love with the sport because a wet suit costs several hundred dollars. Also, triathletes who are experienced swimmers may decide to swim without a wet suit in shorter races because the time it takes to get out of the wet suit can equal or exceed any time they may have saved in the race.

Quick Tips   Use a body lubricant designed to reduce chafing in areas where your wet suit rubs against your body. Common areas include the neck and armpits, especially for sleeveless suits. A second option for protecting potential rub spots is a product called New Skin that acts like a protective layer on top of your skin.

If you wear a wet suit, put the race timing chip underneath the wet suit. (Timing chip timed races issue each racer a numbered chip, typically worn on your ankle. When you cross the timing equipment, the chip triggers the electronic gear and tracks your time.)

Goggles

There are a number of goggle styles available. The main challenges in fitting goggles properly are comfort, leaking, fogging, and field of vision. In the category of comfort, one athlete may find the minimal style of goggles very comfortable. Such goggles feature two plastic cups to cover the eyes, no or minimal padding around the eyepieces, a small nosepiece that is often made of a plastic tube and string, and rubber straps to hold the goggles in place on the head. Most often it is the very experienced swimmer who finds the minimal-style goggles comfortable.

If you prefer more cushioning around your eye socket than that offered by the minimal goggles, there is a large selection available. The first step in selecting goggles is to find some with eyepieces that fit your particular face structure. Some people have deep-set eyes and a narrow nose, while others have a wider nose bridge and shallow eye sockets. The shape of the goggles and the padding around the goggle cups influence fit. It is beneficial to work with a good salesperson who can help you sort through the various models to find your best option.

In addition to considering fit, you might want to consider other goggle options, such as tinted lenses, prescription lenses, and lenses made of prescription-quality material. Some lenses even have a special coating to prevent fogging or special tinting to reflect the sun.

Some athletes prefer a mask instead of goggles for the added peripheral vision and decreased pressure on the eye sockets and the bridge of the nose that a mask offers. The masks designed for swimming or triathlon are lighter and more hydrodynamic than scuba or snorkel masks.

Quick Tips A small amount of no-tears baby shampoo in your goggles can prevent fogging. Mix equal parts of shampoo with water in a small container. (An empty eyedrop container works well. Just pry the top off after the eyedrops are gone and fill with your no-fog solution.) Put a drop of the solution into each goggle cup and smear it around with your finger. Dunk the goggle in the pool a couple of times or rinse with fresh water from your water bottle to eliminate excess soap. Too much soap may irritate your eyes, while too little will not prevent fogging.

Putting your cap on over your goggle strap helps prevent your goggles from being pulled off during an open-water swim.

Quick Tip   Keep two pairs of goggles in your swim and race bag.

Swimming Pool Toys—Fins, Buoys, and Paddles

Fins, buoys, and paddles can be useful training tools. Be careful to use these tools to complement your training and not as constant crutches. Fins can improve ankle flexibility, isolate work on your kick, and be used as sport-specific strength training for the swim kick. Pull buoys are flotation devices placed between your legs to help you keep a prone body position when not using your kick. Buoys are useful tools for isolating upper body training and can help you work on good body roll. Adding paddles while using pull buoys offers sport-specific strength training for swimming. Because paddles can put additional pressure on the shoulders, they are not recommended for beginning swimmers. When you decide to add paddles to your workout mix, begin by using them for 100 to 200 yards or meters and build from there.

Quick Tip   Wearing light socks with fins can eliminate blisters and hot spots on your feet.

Bike

If you scan the transition area of beginner-friendly triathlons, you will find a wide range of bicycle types. For your first triathlon, any bicycle you have will work fine. After the triathlon bug bites, you may want to consider a new bicycle. The right bicycle can improve your triathlon experience.

The two areas where the right bicycle can have the most impact are comfort and speed. If a bicycle fits correctly, you are more likely to enjoy cycling and find it easy to spend time riding. A good fit also reduces the likelihood of cycling-related injuries.

Finding a comfortable fit is one reason athletes shop for a new bike. The second reason is to gain speed or a faster bike split. The right bike can make a significant difference in your bike time. The big question is, Which bike is the right bike?

Before you can answer that question, you need to know what makes bicycles different from one another. Let's begin with the basics.

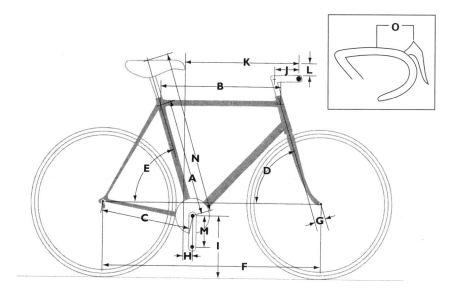

Figure 2.1 **Road Bike Measurements**

A' Seat tube length, measured center-to-center
A" Seat tube length, measured center-to-top
B   Top tube length
C   Chainstay length
D   Head tube angle
E   Seat tube angle
F   Wheel base
G   Fork offset
H   Seat setback
I   Bottom bracket height
J   Stem length
K   Saddle to transverse centerline of handlebar
L   Seat to handlebar drop
M   Crank
N' Seat height, measured from bottom bracket centerline
    (also shown in Figure 2.9)
N" Seat height, measured from pedal spindle
    (not shown here, shown in Figure 2.10)
O   Transverse centerline of handlebar to brake hood

Frame Geometry and Bike Purpose

The most common bicycles found in a typical race transition area are road bikes, mountain bikes, hybrid bikes, and triathlon bikes. As the race becomes more competitive, such as USA Triathlon National Championships or Ironman®, the majority of bicycles in the transition area are triathlon bikes and a few road bikes. What are the differences between bicycles?

A bicycle designed for the road, often called a road bike, has skinny tires and frame geometry intended for road riding. The frame geometry measurement people talk about most often is the seat–tube angle, dimension E on Figure 2.1. A road bike seat–tube angle typically ranges from about 73 to 75 degrees. Mountain and hybrid bikes usually have tires wider than those found on a road bike and seat–tube angles that range from just over 71 to as steep as 75 degrees. The lower seat–tube angles found on these bikes are considered to constitute a more "relaxed" frame geometry. Mountain bikes are designed for heavy off-road riding, single track, going over rocks and other trail obstacles. Hybrid bikes are designed for road and light off-road riding, such as dirt roads with few technical obstacles.

Triathlon or time trial–specific frames have skinny tires like those on a road bike and are intended for road use. The most noticeable differences between a triathlon bike and a road bike are that the former has aerobars instead of regular handlebars and many models have specially shaped frame tubing and special wheels. These design features are intended to minimize drag and increase speed (more on this later). Triathlon bikes have steeper seat–tube angles that range from around 75 to 80 degrees. Photographs of the different bicycles are shown in Figures 2.2–2.5.

Bicycle geometry affects the handling and comfort of the bike. A bicycle created for a time trial purpose, such as non-drafting triathlon, handles differently from a bike designed for multiple-day bike tours. A bike designed to tour across the country, carrying panniers or packs on both sides of the back wheel, needs yet different design features than a bike designed for racing criteriums. (Criteriums are short-course road races, with multiple corners taken at high speeds in a group or pack riding situation.) Some questions you need to answer before purchasing your next bike are:

Figure 2.2 **Road bikes** have skinny tires, handlebars with drops, fingertips shifters, and may or may not have aerodynamic wheels.

What is the purpose of this bike and for what will I use it?

Is this new bicycle the only one you will own or will you own more than one bicycle?

Will triathlon become your sole focus or do you intend to do a good deal of road riding or racing, including on very hilly courses?

Do your plans include participation in organized century rides and multiple-day bike tours?

For beginning endurance athletes looking for a single bike to serve multiple purposes, I recommend a road bike. Road bike geometry is much better suited for multipurpose riding, including bike tours, hilly courses, and an occasional sprint or Olympic distance triathlon. The big reasons for this recommendation are comfort and performance. The geometry of a road frame is better suited for group riding and climbing hills, and the drop bars offer more hand positions to make riding comfortable.

Figure 2.3 **Mountain bikes** have wider tires than a road bike, handlebars that are straight across (no drops), shocks on the front wheel, and sometimes rear shocks as well.

Figure 2.4 **Hybrid bikes** often have wider tires than a road bike, yet narrower than a mountain bike. The handlebars do not have drops and the rider sits more upright than on a road bike. These bikes can be taken off-road, but do not have the durability of a mountain bike. Some hybrids have shocks.

Figure 2.5 **Triathlon or time trial bikes** often have frames and wheels that are aerodynamic. The handlebars have elbow pads so the rider can rest in an aerodynamic (aero) position. When riding in an aero position, shift levers are at the rider's fingertips. Brakes are located about halfway between the elbow pads and the bar-end shifters.

The two hand positions most often used while road riding are on the brake hoods and on the top of the handlebars. These positions put the rider upright and are more comfortable for many people. Note that while the positions are comfortable, they are not aerodynamic.

To make yourself "more aerodynamic" means taking measures to more easily slip through the air while riding your bicycle. You want to reduce drag or the resistance to forward progress. Your position on the bicycle, the bicycle design, and components on the bicycle have the greatest effect on reducing drag.

Recall that riding on the brake hoods is a comfortable road riding position. Changing a rider's position from the brake hoods to using aerobars makes the rider more aerodynamic. Figures 2.6 and 2.7 show the difference between a road position and an aerodynamic position. Getting into an aerodynamic

Figure 2.6 Touring Position on a Road Bike

Figure 2.7 Aerodynamic Position on a Triathlon Bike

position on a flat or rolling course considerably reduces the rider's power output. For an elite cyclist pedaling at 25 miles per hour, changing her position from the brake hoods to aerobars reduces the power required to maintain her speed by 20 percent. This is a significant reduction in power. The same speed for less power output also means more speed for the same power output. This is why a triathlon or time trial bike, complete with aerobars, is attractive for non-drafting races. If the aerobars make such a big difference, how about just putting aerobars on a road bike?

Mounting the short, clip-on aerobars on a road bike is a good option if you plan to do limited sprint and Olympic distance events and you have only a road bike. The short, clip-on aerobars are the style used by many of the elite athletes doing draft-legal racing. Although they do offer an aerodynamic advantage, some of the short aerobars do not have elbow pads and they are not the most comfortable option for long distance racing.

Full aerobars, complete with elbow pads and shifters located at your fingertips, are the best aerodynamic option for non-drafting triathlon. Elbow pads make the ride comfortable and with the shifters at your fingertips, you can minimize the number of times you sit up and create a sail to catch the wind with your chest. One problem with modifying your current road bike, by adding aerobars complete with elbow pads and fingertip shifting, is that it compromises your position and the handling characteristics of the bike. In the worst case, the compromise reduces your power output on the bike, makes your bike handling dangerous, and puts you in a position that creates the potential of an injury.

The compromises in comfort, handling, and performance come from needing to move your entire body forward on the bike in order to rest on the elbow pads. Sometimes moving your seat all the way forward and installing the shortest stem to hold the aerobars are not enough to keep you from being too stretched out on the bike. Often the elbow pads end up in the center of your forearm, definitely an uncomfortable position. Stretching your body out with the support point under the midsection of your forearm causes arm, neck, and shoulder pain. Seldom can full aerobars be added to a road bike and result in an optimal situation.

If you have the luxury of owning two bicycles, it is best to have a road bike and a triathlon-specific bike. The road bike is used for some training and group riding situations. The triathlon bike is used for some training and all triathlon racing.

If you plan to own one bicycle and triathlon training and racing are your only passion—no group riding, hilly rides, or multiday tours—a triathlon bike is the best option.

In all the bicycle categories, you can find a wide range of prices for a new ride. Adding the following options will increase a bike's price: lightweight frame material, special aerodynamic frame design, aerodynamic wheels, lightweight components, high-quality components that resist wear with higher volumes of training, or new technical advances in design. However, the most expensive bike in the world is useless for your training and racing if it does not fit.

Quick Tips Pump your tires to the full recommended pressure before each ride. Tires that are low require more exertion by the rider to go any given pace.

Some tubes and tires lose as much as 10 psi just sitting in your garage overnight. Pump the tires before each ride so that you can ride faster for less effort.

Do not inflate your tires beyond the pressure recommended by the manufacturer. (This pressure level is embossed on the tire wall.) Inflating tires beyond the pressure recommended by the manufacturer can cause tire failure and perhaps injury to the rider.

Bike Fit

In 1998, when I began work on my first book, *The Female Cyclist: Gearing up a Level*, it was common knowledge in popular cycling literature that women have shorter torsos than men do. I did not find a single document in cycling that was contrary to this belief. Assuming this short-torso issue for women was fact, I thought it would be fun to include anatomical drawings of the male and female bodies in the book to display the differences. When I began searching for data to support the notion that women have shorter torsos than men, I found none.

What I found is that there is little difference in the ratio of torso or leg length to overall height when comparing male and female body data. When looking at the gross data, given a male and a female of equal heights and relatively equal leg lengths, the major fit concerns are arm reach to the hoods or drops and hand size, affecting reach to the brake levers. When data on 64-inch males and females are compared, the arm length for women is, on average, shorter by 2 inches. In addition to having shorter arms, women tend to have smaller hands than men of their same height.

To examine the differences between the genders, comparing a 64-inch man and woman works well. However, the average height for men in the data is 69 inches, compared with the average height of women at 64 inches. When *The Female Cyclist* was written, most bicycles were manufactured to meet the needs of the "average" user. The average cyclist used to be an average-sized male. Since that time, great changes have taken place. The multisport and cycling population has grown in size and diversity. This growth has created a demand for recreational and high-performance bicycles for people of all sizes. Because equipment is available to make cycling more comfortable, more people are attracted to cycling. This is an excellent synergistic relationship.

Finding a Bike That Fits

Finding a bike that fits is critical. The "right" bike means one that offers comfort, reduced likelihood of injury, and more power—which translates to more speed. The right bike with a good fit requires more than standing over the top tube and looking for 1 to 2 inches of clearance. Let's look at the important considerations for determining if a bike fits you.

Frame Size—Road Bike, Regular Geometry

Figure 2.1 shows some of the anatomy and geometry of a standard bicycle. (See the next section on compact geometry.) Learning the proper terms is helpful in the quest to purchase a bicycle.

Bicycle size is typically given in centimeters and refers to the length of the seat tube. A 54-centimeter (cm) bike has a 54-cm seat tube. Frames are measured in two ways, center-to-top and center-to-center. Center-to-top measures the distance from the center of the bottom bracket to the top of the top tube or seat lug. Center-to-center measures from the center of the bottom bracket to the center of the top tube at the seat lug. The center-to-center measurement is about 1.0 to 1.5 cm smaller than the center-to-top measure. Be aware of this when you compare frames.

Frame sizes in the 50 to 60 cm range are easy to find. Some manufacturers make 49, 48, and even smaller frames to 43 cm. Small frames often have 650-cm wheels. These smaller wheels keep your foot and the front tire from interfering with each other on tight turns.

A rule of thumb for selecting a road bike frame is to begin the selection by standing over the bicycle in stocking feet and lifting the bicycle until the top tube is snug in your crotch. There should be 1 to 2 inches of clearance between the tires and the floor. Riding a frame that is either too large or too small compromises performance and handling, and it can put you at risk for injury.

As noted previously in this chapter, different bike styles may have different seat–tube angles. The most common road bike seat–tube angle of 73 to 75 degrees allows the "average" cyclist to position his knee over the pedal axle, with minor adjustments in the fore and aft position of the saddle.

The next consideration when selecting a frame size is the length of the top tube. Top tubes are typically within plus or minus 2 cm of the seat tube length. A guideline to use is to divide your height by your inseam length, as measured in Figure 2.8. If that value is 2.0 to 2.2, you are considered average and a frame that has a top tube equal to the seat tube would fit you. If your value is greater than 2.2, you have a long torso and a longer top tube may be what you need. Less than 2.0 indicates your torso is short, in comparison with your legs, and you are better off with a top tube that is shorter than the seat tube.

For example, if a person's inseam is 32.5 inches and height is 64.5 inches, the ratio is 64.5 divided by 32.5, equaling 1.99. He is just under the 2.0 guideline. He may be able to ride an average frame, depending on the length of his arms. If his arms are not considered to be long, they may be more comfortable on a frame where the top tube is shorter than the seat tube.

The ratio value is most applicable to average-size riders, says custom frame builder Lennard Zinn. "Smaller riders always need top tubes longer than the seat tube, and vice versa for very tall riders. This is

Figure 2.8 **Inseam Measurement with a Level:** Using a carpenter's level that is 2 to 3 feet long, stand in stocking feet on a flat, hard surface and snug the level into your crotch. The pressure between the level and your crotch (how much force you apply upward) should be similar to the pressure between a bicycle seat and your crotch. Have an assistant tell you when the level is parallel to the floor and have him measure the distance from the floor to the top of the level. This value is the inseam length.

because the top tube length is a proportional measurement, whereas the seat tube length is produced by subtraction and is dependent on crank length, seat post extension, and saddle dimensions, which are similar regardless of the rider."

Top tube and seat tube lengths vary between manufacturers and within the product line of a single manufacturer. The ratio values given in previous paragraphs do not apply to a "compact" geometry bicycle.

Frame Size: Road Bike, Compact Geometry

The discussion about top tube length in the previous section applies to a regular-geometry bicycle, or one where the top tube is parallel to the ground. Compact-geometry bicycles have top tubes that angle toward the ground. Some manufacturers make compact sizes in small, medium, and large sizing. Other manufacturers size according to the seat tube, center-to-top measurement. You may have more stand-over clearance between your crotch and the top tube on these bikes. Check the manufacturer catalogues for seat tube, top tube, and effective top tube measurement differences. "Effective top tube measurement" refers to the length of an imaginary parallel-to-the-ground top tube.

Seat Height

There are several ways to estimate seat height. If you already have a bike and you know the seat height is correct, take the measurement with you to the bike shop (shown in Figure 2.1). If you aren't sure what the correct seat height is, you can estimate it by taking your inseam measurement from Figure 2.8 and multiplying by 0.883. The product of those two numbers is the distance from the center of the bottom bracket to the top of the saddle, as in Figure 2.9.

Your crank length and type of pedal and shoe used will influence seat height. If you use toe clips, the seat height method mentioned in the previous paragraph is close to what you need. If you use clipless pedals, you may have to adjust the seat height measurement around 3 mm. How much you adjust the value depends on your shoe, cleat, and pedal combination and how far that combination stacks your foot above the pedal axle. Seat height is also affected by muscle flexibility. Low flexibility may

Figure 2.9 **Seat Height Measurement from Center of Bottom Bracket:** The distance from the center of the bottom bracket to the top of the saddle, measured along a line connecting the bottom bracket to the point where the rider's crotch will rest on the saddle, is one way to measure seat height.

Figure 2.10 **Seat Height Measurement from Top of Pedal Spindle:** The distance from the top of the pedal spindle to the top of the saddle. You can also take this measurement along a line that connects the spindle to the point where the rider's crotch will rest on the saddle. This particular method is helpful when changing crank lengths or saddles. When changing saddles or cranks, be certain the saddle height remains the same, otherwise discomfort or injury may result.

require a lower seat. If you decide to change your current seat height, make changes slowly, only about an eighth to a quarter inch per week.

A second and easy way to estimate seat height is to sit on the bike while it is mounted in a stationary trainer. A quality bicycle shop will put the bicycle in a trainer to help you arrive at the correct bicycle setup. On the trainer, pedal the bike at a seat height that seems comfortable. Unclip your cleats from the pedal system, put your heels on the top of the pedals, and pedal backward. The seat should be placed at a height that allows you to keep your heels on the pedals while pedaling backward and does not allow your hips to rock from side to side. When you are clipped into the pedals and begin to pedal forward again, you should have a slight bend in your knee, about 25 to 30 degrees.

Some visual cues that indicate the correct height include "quiet hips" and knees that align with your feet and hips. With the bicycle in the trainer, pedal for a few moments until you are settled and comfortable with your riding position. Then, continue to pedal and have someone look at your hips from the rear. Your hips should have a slight rocking motion, but it should not be excessive. Excessive rocking, as if you are straining to reach the bottom of every pedal stroke, indicates your seat is too high.

While pedaling, a view from the front should reveal your knees tracking in a straight line from your hips to the pedal. Minimal side-to-side motion of your knees is normal. Knees that travel far outside a straight line from the hip to the pedal may signify the seat is too low. If the seat height is correct, excessive movement of the knees from side to side may show the need for orthotics. Also, some people are bowlegged and this should be taken into consideration when watching knee tracking.

Some athletes have anatomical features that may require special adjustments. People with very wide hips may need to have spacers added to their pedal spindles to better align their feet with their hips. Others may have a pedaling motion that when viewed from the rear seems uneven. It may appear as though they are "limping" on the bike. This may indicate a leg length difference. Modifications can be made to the bike to accommodate leg length differences, including spacers in the shoe or on the cleat and fore/aft positioning of the cleat on the pedals. If you suspect you have some anatomy issues that are causing you problems on the bike, it is best to seek the help of a qualified professional, such as a sports medicine physician. They can take x-rays, physical measurements, and make physical examinations to determine if you have anatomical abnormalities.

> **Quick Tip** Cycling shorts are designed to be worn without underwear. If you wear undies with your cycling shorts, the seams can create saddle sores. (Also, other cyclists and triathletes will think you are nerdy if you wear undies!)

Pedals

Clipless pedals are the pedals of choice for most competitive triathletes and road cyclists. Pedals that allow some rotation may prevent injury by allowing your foot to "float" instead of being "fixed." It is commonly thought that a pedal that allows for some knee and foot travel minimizes the risk of injury.

No matter which type of pedal you choose, a guideline is to position the ball of your foot over the pedal axle. When the ball of your foot is ahead of the pedal axle, the lever arm from your ankle to the pedal axle is shortened and puts less stress on your Achilles tendon and calf muscles. If you have problems with Achilles tendon or calf tightness, you can consider moving the ball of your foot ahead of the axle. In this position, you will need less force to stabilize your foot. Time trial specialists and some triathletes use this position because they can produce more force while using larger gears.

If the ball of your foot is behind the pedal axle, it lengthens the ankle to pedal-axle lever arm. Some track cyclists prefer this position because it allows a higher cadence during fixed-gear events, but few triathletes use this position.

> **Quick Tip** You can leave your shoes attached to the pedals on race day. This means running in bare feet from your transition area to the bike mount line. A small amount of powder in each shoe helps them go on wet feet easier.

Quick Tip   Keeping your chain lubricated and clean reduces friction. This translates to less effort to pedal the bicycle at any given speed. It also makes changing a rear flat tire less messy.

Saddle Position

While on the stationary trainer, pedal the bicycle until you feel settled. Once settled, stop pedaling and put the crank arms horizontal to the ground, in the three and nine o'clock positions, as shown in Figure 2.11. Your feet should be horizontal or as close to horizontal as your flexibility allows. A neutral foot position has the front of your knee in line with the front of the crank arm. The position can be measured with a common yardstick, a wooden dowel, a sturdy piece of 1-inch-by-1-inch lumber, or a carpenter's level. Whatever you use, be certain the measuring tool remains perpendicular to the ground and does not bend beneath the measuring pressure.

Some triathletes and time trial specialists prefer to position the knee slightly forward of the neutral position. Remember that if you slide the seat (also called a saddle) forward on the rails, you are, in effect, lowering seat height. If you adjust the saddle forward, fine-tune the seat height higher, or increase the measure shown in Figure 2.9. A rule of thumb is, for every centimeter you move the seat forward, raise the seat post a half-centimeter.

The saddle should be level or parallel to the ground for general riding purposes. If the saddle nose is pointed downward, athletes tend to put more pressure on their upper body, because they are trying to keep from sliding forward. Athletes who feel the need to have the nose of the saddle pointed down probably have their seat too high or perhaps handlebars too low. If you decide to tilt the nose of your saddle downward a degree or two, be certain you are not constantly pushing yourself back onto the saddle. This constant body adjustment is a recipe for loss of power and speed, in addition to sore and bruised body parts.

A few athletes prefer to tilt the nose of the saddle up. If you do this, be certain there is no pressure on your genital area, causing pain, saddle sores, or numbing.

You can use a carpenter's level to ensure your saddle is parallel with the ground. Have someone hold your bike in the riding position, while you

Figure 2.11 **Knee in Relation to Crank Arm** (with an assistant): To measure with a common yardstick, the yardstick should touch the knee and align with the end of the crank arm. The assistant can make certain the yardstick is perpendicular to the ground.

check seat tilt. If you check seat tilt while the bike is on a stationary trainer, be certain it is level and both tires are raised off the ground equally.

Quick Tip   If you race in a swimsuit, a small amount of body lubricant applied to the nose of the bike saddle can keep your legs from chafing on it. Also, extra lubricant can be stored under the saddle nose. Know that if the saddle is glued together, some lubricants can destroy the glue.

Figure 2.12 **Knee in Relation to Crank Arm** (self-measurement): To measure your own knee in relation to the crank arm, loop a plumb line around your leg. The plumb line should drop from the front of the knee and align with the end of the crank arm. A plumb line can be constructed with a lightweight nylon string and a nut, available at most hardware stores.

Stem

The position of your knee over the pedal is important. Do not compromise this position in an attempt to reach the handlebars. A common mistake is to move the seat forward to accommodate a short arm reach or to accommodate the addition of aerobars to an otherwise good-fitting road bike. If your arm reach is short, in most cases the stem on the bicycle can easily be changed.

Along the same line, do not use a longer stem to compensate for a frame size that is too small. If you need a stem length beyond about 14 cm or shorter than 6 cm, it is an indication your top tube length is incorrect. The lengths most often used are 11 to 13 cm.

Figure 2.13 **Stem Height:** Using one straightedge, such as a yardstick, touch the saddle and hold the yardstick parallel to the ground. (You could also use a carpenter's level.) Using a second ruler, measure the distance from the bottom of the first straightedge to the top of the handlebars.

One method to determine if your stem length is correct is to pedal the bicycle while it is in a stationary trainer. Again, pedal until you feel settled. With your hands in the drops, in your comfortable cycling position, your stem length is correct if the front wheel axle is blocked from view by the top transverse part of the handlebars. A second way to measure the correct position is to have a friend drop a plumb line from your nose to the ground, while you look forward, settled in your comfortable riding position. The plumb line should intersect the center of your handlebar.

The amount of stem post visible affects the height of your handlebars. This distance can be measured by using the same tool you used to measure your knee position over your crank arm. Lay the straightedge across your saddle and have someone measure the distance from the straightedge to the top of your handlebars, as shown in Figure 2.13. Typically, handlebars are about 1 to 2 inches below the top of the saddle. Some tall people or those with long arms go as much as 4 inches below the top of the saddle.

Typically, lowering the stem puts your body in a more aerodynamic position. To be comfortable in a lower position, you need flexible hamstrings and an ability to rotate your pelvis. Signs that your stem may be too low are pain or numbness in the genital area; quadriceps hitting your torso on each pedal stroke; neck, shoulder, or arm pain; and hand numbness.

Raising the stem puts you in a more upright riding position and can take some of the pressure off the areas mentioned in the previous paragraph, where you are experiencing pain or numbness. A high stem, however, opens your chest area to catching more wind and is less aerodynamic. There is a mark on the stem post that warns you not to raise the stem beyond that line. Raising the stem beyond the line risks damage to the head tube or breaking the stem post.

Handlebars and Brake Levers

The width of the handlebars is roughly the same width as your shoulders. Handlebar widths are different and can be changed to suit your anatomy. Typically, handlebars are either level with the road or rotated slightly up, so the handlebar ends point toward the rear hub.

If you happen to have small hands, consider "short reach" brake levers such as those manufactured by Shimano.

Crank Length

Most beginning athletes purchase stock frames that come with standard crank arms. If the speed-bug bites you and you begin researching ways to get faster, crank arm length is a factor that will continue to surface. It is a much-debated topic when it comes to optimizing performance.

Longer cranks have a mechanical advantage and are better for pushing larger gears, such as in time trialing. This can translate to more power and speed. Keep in mind, however, that the crank arm length influences cadence, can cause extra stress on the knees, and affects saddle height. A switch to longer cranks may mean you need to lower your seat in order to keep your hips from rocking at the bottom of the pedal stroke. Once your seat height is properly adjusted to longer cranks, the change may cause interference between your quadriceps and torso, which is certainly not optimal.

Optimizing crank arm length is not covered in detail in this book. One good resource on this topic, and other bicycle topics, is equipment expert and legendary frame builder Lennard Zinn. You can find crank information on his Web site at www.zinncycles.com/cranks.aspx. He has also written a book with extensive information on bicycle fit, *Zinn's Cycling Primer: Maintenance Tips and Skill Building for Cyclists.*

Saddles

Saddle style is probably the most intimate and frustrating element of bike fit. No saddle is going to make up for an ill-fitting bicycle, and no one wants to ride any distance if his private parts are in pain or have gone numb. Saddles come in various styles, lengths, and widths to accommodate individual anatomies. Whether you prefer a wide or narrow seat, minimal padding or a gel insert, a solid seat or a seat with a cutout depends on your riding style, the length of time you spend in the saddle, your anatomy, and personal preferences. The saddles touted as "women's models" tend to be wider and shorter. Many men also find these wider saddles suit their anatomy just fine and eliminate genital numbness (and allay fears about impotence). However, "women's saddles" are limited in their fore-aft adjustment range.

Some saddle discomfort can be caused by fitness level and riding style. Novice cyclists do not have the leg and gluteus muscles of an experienced cyclist. Strong leg muscles help support a cyclist so the saddle does not become a chair. Novice cyclists who have not developed strong leg muscles tend to "sit" on the saddle and move their legs, while experienced cyclists are somewhat suspended by their legs. The message for the novice is to slowly build cycling miles in order to build leg strength and saddle time. Even experienced cyclists need to build saddle time after being off the bike for a while.

It is important that a saddle be padded for comfort. However, too much padding and/or padding that is very pliable can also cause numbness. If the saddle has too much padding that is pliable, over the course of a ride the padding can get reshaped and move into the perineum, which is the area between your sit bones. That area has arteries and nerves running through it, which, when compressed, can cause pain.

Unfortunately, there is no easy sizing system for saddles. It would be great if they were like shoe sizes, having length and width designations such as "I'll need a size eight in a C width." Until that happens, test different saddles to find one that is comfortable. Good bicycle shops will mount your bike on a stationary trainer and let you try a few saddles before you buy one. If you ask around, you're likely to find saddle choice is a bit like ice cream flavors; everyone has a favorite for different reasons.

Custom Frame?

There is no easy way to determine if you need a custom frame or not. That formula, yet undeveloped, is a function of overall height in addition to the ratio of leg length, torso length, and arm length to height. Custom frame maker Lennard Zinn says people who are on the low and high ends of the anatomy spectrum might consider a custom frame. Generally speaking, those under 5'3" or over 6'4" with an inseam over 36 inches are good candidates for a custom frame. So are those people who have trouble getting a normal frame to fit due to abnormally short or long torsos.

Triathlon or Time Trial Positions

If you are reading this book, it's fair to assume that you are interested in non-drafting triathlons. The bicycle leg of a non-drafting triathlon is an individual time trial, for which aerodynamics is a big concern. To reduce the effect of wind drag, you want to be as compact as possible. While some athletes seek a knowledgeable professional to help them on this issue, others prefer to do it on their own.

If you decide to evaluate and make changes to body position on your own, a good tool is a camera. Set your bike up on a trainer and have a willing assistant take photos or, better yet, movies of you pedaling. Take a shot from the front, both sides, and the back. Getting an aerodynamic position means getting your body position low on the bike. From a front view, your arms are about shoulder width apart. While pedaling, your knees are in line with your feet and hip joints. In other words, your knees do not protrude outward or inward on each pedal stroke. From a rear view, knees, ankles, and hips should all track in a line perpendicular to the ground.

From a side view while in the aero position, your back is relatively flat. Know that some people have a natural hump in their backs, which means their backs will never appear totally flat. While pedaling and looking down the road in a riding position, if a line is drawn from your ear perpendicular to the ground, that line runs through your elbow. All these adjustments need to be made without sacrificing safety or comfort.

Riding in an aerodynamic position using aerobars may take some time to accomplish. Resting on your forearms affects steering responsiveness and balance. Riding with a flat back requires flexible back and hamstring muscles, as well as a rotation of the pelvis forward. This forward rotation and new position may put added pressure on genitals. A seat that has a portion of the nose relieved or gel padding on the nose may help relieve pressure.

Quick Tips Keep your head up and look ahead a good distance so you can anticipate trouble. Too often, triathletes put their heads down and look at a spot about 2 feet ahead of the front tire. This is dangerous for the rider and anyone else nearby.

Ride in a straight line. Weaving from side to side with every pedal stroke wastes energy and speed.

If you need to take your bike on an airplane, know there is an additional baggage charge. This charge can be in excess of $100. Some athletes package and ship their bikes by United Parcel Service. While the bike does not travel with you, the shipping charge is typically lower than the airline charge. Check your options prior to travel.

Quick Tips For a first race, many athletes wear socks. To reduce transition time, some athletes choose not to put on socks. If you decide to go sockless on race day, practice it during training. It is particularly important for running. If your shoes rub on your feet, use a lubricant on the "hot spots" when you are setting up your gear in the transition area. If your shoe pinches your foot between the insole or orthotic and the upper of the shoe, run a piece of duct tape across the pinch zone.

Do not mow the lawn or do other chores in your running shoes. Use them for running only. Keep track of the miles or hours logged on your running shoes to help you decide when it is time to buy a new pair.

Run

If you are not currently a runner, purchasing your first pair of running shoes can be confusing. There are shoes for racing, running trails, heavy runners, runners needing stability, runners needing cushioning … argh! How do you know what you need if you have never run before?

A good way to begin the process of finding the right shoe is to visit a reputable running shoe dealer in your area. A good dealer can help you find a modestly priced pair of shoes to get you started. She should ask you about your running experience and any problems you have with your feet. After a series of questions, she will begin with one pair of shoes and have you test them. Some dealers have a treadmill in the store and they can watch you walk and run before making further recommendations. At a minimum, the dealer should have you put the shoes on and give them a test walk and jog.

It is best to test new shoes in the afternoon, because your feet tend to swell about a half size over the course of the day and during running. To try new shoes, wear the socks you plan to run in. When you stand up, there should be about the width of your thumb between the tip of your longest toe and the end of the shoe. There should be plenty of room in the toe box to allow up and down movement of your toes. If one of your toes is hitting the top of the shoe, count on a blister forming in that spot while you run. While you do not want the shoe to be too tight and rubbing on your toes, a shoe that is too loose and that slips on your heel can cause blisters, too. The shoes should be comfortable as soon as you put them on and go for a walk.

As you log running miles, your shoes exhibit wear patterns. These wear patterns can help your shoe dealer give you better recommendations for the model of shoe that is best for you. Below are some wear pattern and shoe anatomy terms that can help when you are shoe shopping.

Wear Patterns on the Bottom of Shoes

Normal: A normal wear pattern is when the heel of the shoe wears on the lateral side, or the same side as the small toe. The wear near the front of the shoe is roughly underneath the first two toes and extends to the front of the shoe.

Over-Pronator: The wear pattern on the heel is on the medial side, or the same side as your big toe. This wear extends along a good deal of the shoe up to the toe area, with more wear toward the medial side of the shoe.

Over-Supinator: The wear pattern on the heels is on the lateral side, or the same side as your small toe, and tends to be more on the outside of the shoe. The wear extends along a good deal of the shoe up to the toe area, with more wear toward the lateral side of the shoe.

Quick Tip   Experiencing small aches and pains in your legs, not associated with an increase in mileage or intensity, can mean it is time to replace your running shoes.

Basic Shoe Anatomy

Outer Sole: This is the where the rubber meets the road. The outer sole comes in contact with the ground.

Midsole: The midsole is located next to the outer sole and gives the shoe its degree of hardness or softness. Special inserts are often added to the midsole in an attempt to reduce pronation or supination.

Figure 2.14 Heart Rate Transmitter and Receivers

Lasting: There are two types of lasting—board lasting and slip lasting. If the shoe upper, the part that covers your foot and houses the lacing system, is stitched together and glued to the midsole directly and nothing else covers it, it is said to be slip lasted. If a board material overlies it and covers the stitching, it is said to be board lasted. Board lasting design is intended to improve the ability of the shoe to resist pronation.

There are two shapes of lasting—straight and curved. A straight-lasted shoe appears symmetrical when viewed from the bottom. A curve-lasted shoe, as you might imagine, has a curved appearance when viewed from the bottom. Straight-lasted shoes are designed to provide additional midsole support and to improve the ability of the shoe to resist pronation.

Arch Support or Insole: This is the area that comes in contact with your sock or bare foot should you decide to run without socks. Some runners may need to replace this insole with custom-made orthotics if they have foot issues requiring special attention.

Heel Counter: The heel counter is often made of thermoplastic material and extends up the back of the shoe, underneath the lining. The counter can be very stiff or more pliable.

Upper: This is the outside of the shoe most visible by you when wear-ing the shoes. The seams and special features added to the upper should not bend and poke your foot when you are running.

Quick Tip Using lace locks or elastic laces on your racing shoes saves transition time because they eliminate the need to tie your laces. Slip the shoes on and go!

Some running singlets or shirts can cause nipple-chafing for the guys. This becomes a bigger issue as running time increases. Place a couple of Band-Aids™ over the nipples—no kidding—to eliminate the rubbing, or change shirts.

Heart Rate Monitors

In addition to the basic equipment required to swim, bike, and run, a heart rate monitor system is a good investment because it allows you to monitor your body's response to exercise intensity. In Chapter 3, exer-cise intensity is discussed in detail. Each workout in each training plan has a specific purpose. By monitoring your heart rate and rating of per-ceived exertion (RPE), you can achieve the training effect with each training plan's design. One indicator of improving fitness is your capa-bility of increasing the speed you achieve for a given heart rate level. For example, when beginning a training plan, you may find you can hold 14 miles per hour on your bike and your heart rate hangs around 140 beats per minute. As you improve your fitness, this same heart rate of 140 pro-duces speeds greater than 14 miles per hour.

The most basic heart rate monitoring systems include a transmitter chest belt and a receiver worn like a wristwatch. The chest belt senses the electrical signal originating from your heart and sends a signal to the wrist receiver. The heart rate information appears on the receiver.

There are heart rate monitoring systems available for under $100. The more features the heart rate monitor has, the more expensive it is. Most beginners need only the basics of heart rate display and total exercise time. More advanced models include features such as lap timers, individ-ual heart rate zone settings and alarms, interval timers, data collection and analysis tools, speed and distance monitoring, and power monitoring.

References

Bernhardt, Gale. *The Female Cyclist: Gearing up a Level.* Boulder, CO: VeloPress, 1999: 43–69.

Noakes, Tim, M.D. *Lore of Running.* 4th ed. Champaign, IL: Human Kinetics, 2003: 264–71, 763–65.

Chapter 3

Exercise Intensity

At the peak of tremendous and victorious effort ...
while the blood is pounding in your head, all suddenly becomes
quiet within you. Everything seems clearer and whiter than ever before, as if great
spotlights had been turned on. At that moment you have the conviction that you
contain all the power in the world, that you are capable of everything, that you
have wings. There is no more precious moment than this, the white moment,
and you will work very hard for years just to taste it again.
—Yuri Vlasov, Russian weightlifter

For any athlete, beginning or experienced, the volume of available training information can be overwhelming. The task of sorting the important "need to know" information from "nice to know" and "how does this apply to me?" is mind-boggling. Much of the confusion stems from the lack of a single common language among endurance sport coaches or scientists to describe training intensity and workout specifics. Some coaches use distance and pace to describe workouts. Other coaches use time and "rating of perceived exertion" (RPE) or time and heart rate to describe workouts. Still others use a combination of distance, workout time, pace, perceived exertion, heart rate, and, for those

Table 3.1 Reference Scale for Rating of Perceived Exertion (RPE) and Training Zones

Zone	Swim Pace	Percent of LT Heart Rate (Bike)	Percent of LT Heart Rate (Run)	RPE / Borg Scale
1	Work on form, no clock watching.	80 and less	< 84	6–9
2	T-Pace + 10 sec. per 100	81–88	85–91	10–12
3	T-Pace + 5 sec. per 100	89–93	92–95	13–14
4	T-Pace	94–99	96–99	15–16
5a	T-Pace	100–102	100–102	17
5b	T-Pace – 5 sec. per 100	103–105	103–106	18–19
5c	As fast as possible	106+	107+	20

who have access to power meters, prescribed power output. Holy cow, no wonder it is so confusing.

Not all coaches who use heart rate to guide training intensity use the same testing protocol to determine training "zones." Not only is there no agreed-upon common protocol for testing, once the tests are complete there are at least a dozen different ways to interpret the results of laboratory tests and assign training zones.

Laboratory tests? I'm a beginner. I'm not going to be tested at some laboratory. I just want to get through my first triathlon without killing myself, crawling, or losing control of my bodily functions in front of my friends and neighbors. Does training for a triathlon really have to be that complicated?

Breathing and Perception (e.g., running)	Purpose and Cross-reference of Terms Commonly Used to Describe Each Zone
Gentle rhythmic breathing. Pace is easy and relaxed. For running, intensity is a jog or trot.	**Easy, Aerobic, Recovery**
Breathing rate and pace increase slightly. Many notice a change, with slightly deeper breathing, although still comfortable. Running pace remains comfortable and conversations are possible.	**Aerobic, Extensive Endurance, Aerobic Threshold Endurance** (Note: Some coaches call this region "Lactate Threshold." See text for details.)
Aware of breathing a little harder. Pace is moderate. It is more difficult to hold conversation.	**Tempo, Intensive Endurance** Ironman distance race pace for experienced athletes is typically within Zones 1 to 3.
Starting to breathe hard. Pace is fast and beginning to get uncomfortable. Approaching all-out 1-hr. run pace.	**Subthreshold, Muscular Endurance, Threshold Endurance, Anaerobic Threshold Endurance**
Breathing deep and forceful. Many notice a second significant change in breathing pattern. Pace is all-out sustainable for 1–1.5 hr. Mental focus required. Moderately uncomfortable, conversation is undesirable.	**Lactate Threshold Endurance, Anaerobic Threshold Endurance, Superthreshold, Muscular Endurance** Olympic distance race pace is typically Zones 4 to 5a for experienced athletes.
Heavy, labored breathing. Pace is noticeably challenging but sustainable for 15–30 min. Discomfort is high, but manageable.	**Aerobic Capacity, Speed Endurance, Anaerobic Endurance** Sprint distance race pace is typically Zones 4 to 5b, with limited 5c for experienced athletes.
Maximal exertion in breathing. Pace is sprinting effort. High discomfort that is unsustainable for over 1 min.	**Anaerobic Capacity, Power**

No, safely navigating through information to train for your first triathlon does not have to be extremely complicated. The intention of this book is to boil down the training information to some basics you can begin to apply today. It will also give you tools to help you interpret other training advice. Hopefully, at some point you'll outgrow the information in this book and seek to gain more knowledge.

In this book, the training priorities are:

1 Remain healthy. Athletes who are ill or injured can never realize their full potential. This is the number-one goal for beginning and elite athletes alike.

2 Train so you have enough endurance to complete the event comfortably, while minimizing risk of injury or illness. This is best accomplished by focusing on aerobic training, saving speed records for later in your triathlon career.

3 Begin the process of learning about various training intensities and how to relate the science of training to your own situation.

The no-frills method of gauging exercise intensity is "rating of perceived exertion" (RPE). Although it is the least "scientific" method of measurement, it remains a critical tool. How difficult any particular training or racing effort *feels* is important. Table 3.1 gives you some breathing indicators to help guide your training zones. RPE is a good tool to hone as you become a more experienced athlete. Be aware, however, that RPE can lead you astray and have you working harder than you intend. It is common for beginning athletes to underestimate how hard they are working.

The heart rate monitor is a widely used and affordable training tool. It can be used to give us a peek at what's happening inside the body. It is a good "noninvasive" tool, meaning no blood has to be drawn, as with some of the lab tests. Scientists have determined that when athletes are subjected to similar testing conditions, heart rate is a reasonably reliable gauge of energy expenditure within the body. To help you interpret heart rate data and laboratory test results, a good first step is to understand your body's energy production mechanisms.

Energy Production

Our bodies need to receive a continuous supply of energy—even for sleep. Energy is supplied by complex chemical reactions. The end result of these chemical reactions is a rich compound called adenosine triphosphate or ATP. The potential energy within the ATP molecule is utilized by your body for all energy-burning processes of the cells. Your body uses two basic methods to produce ATP. One method is aerobic, or with oxygen, and the second method is anaerobic, or without the presence of oxygen. The method of energy production your body uses depends on the rate of demand for energy, the intensity of the demand, and the length or duration of the demand for energy. During short bursts of high-speed activity, the anaerobic system of energy production fuels the muscles. For longer efforts, fat and glycogen are burned aerobically to create ATP.

A small amount of energy is readily available in the body to be utilized "on demand." For example, when you sprint to make it through an intersection before the light changes, you need a small burst of energy instantly. The majority of the energy necessary for this sprint is created anaerobically. You may notice a burning sensation in your legs after you have finished your sprinting. After ending the sprint, you move at a slower speed and energy is once again generated mostly by aerobic means.

For short sprints, energy is created anaerobically and uses ATP stored in the muscle cells to complete the work. ATP is stored in the cells in limited quantities. It is readily available, but is used quickly. A second method of anaerobic energy production involves glycogen and lactic acid. A very fast race, such as a 5k running race, uses large amounts of stored glycogen at a very fast rate. This kind of race uses anaerobic and aerobic energy metabolism. Aerobically produced ATP, on the other hand, takes more time for the body to produce, but is available in huge quantities. These large quantities of energy enable an athlete to exercise for several hours at easy to moderate speeds.

The energy production system within the body is quite complex, and the preceding discussion barely scratches the surface. It is important to note that although an athlete may be swimming, cycling, or running at an easy to moderate pace, some portion of the energy it takes to do so is produced anaerobically. In other words, both energy production systems are working simultaneously. As the intensity or speed of exertion increases, the body requires higher levels of energy that are produced at a faster pace. Recall that the aerobic system needs time to produce energy and is not as quick as the anaerobic system. The bottom line is, as the pace of activity increases, the body increases anaerobic energy production to provide energy until the rate of demand exceeds the rate of production.

One of the by-products of the anaerobic energy production system is lactic acid. Lactic acid is often viewed as an evil demon, but in fact it is another energy source for the body. When given enough time, the body can process and use lactic acid to produce ATP. Lactate is present in the blood at rest. Even as you sit and read this book, low levels of lactate are circulating in your bloodstream. Scientists can measure the amount of lactate present in the body by taking blood samples. At rest, healthy persons have lactate values measuring between 1 and 2 millimoles per liter (mmol/L) of blood. In comparison, when in a recovered state, elite-trained distance runners have resting lactate values around 0.3 to 0.6 mmol/L.

At low levels, lactic acid is not a problem. As you continue to increase your workout intensity, your body increases energy production, relying more heavily on anaerobic metabolism. Greater reliance on anaerobic metabolism causes the lactate level in your blood to rise. With gentle increases in exercise intensity, the lactate level tends to increase at a linear rate. As exercise intensity continues to increase, even though the increase might be gradual, your body can no longer process lactic acid fast enough and lactate is produced at an exponential rate. In other words, lactate begins accumulating faster than your body can process it. In this book, the estimated point where exponential lactate accumulation begins is referred to as "lactate threshold." Other terms for lactate threshold are anaerobic threshold, lactate turn point, second threshold, and onset of blood lactate accumulation to 4 mmol. (Some laboratories mark lactate threshold when lactate measures 4 mmol/L.) This accumulation is closely correlated with heart rate and ventilatory (breathing) rate. Athletes can often tell when they have reached lactate threshold because their breathing becomes labored and some while later they begin to feel a "burning" sensation in their muscles. It is important to note that the burning sensation can lag behind ventilatory threshold by several minutes. More about this later.

If athletes exceed lactate threshold pace by a large margin, they can only sustain their increased pace for a few minutes before the discomfort forces them to slow down. The margin by which lactate threshold is exceeded is inversely proportional to the time the athlete is able to sustain that pace. In other words, if an athlete's estimated lactate threshold heart rate is 162 and the heart rate is pushed to 172, he or she can hold that pace for a shorter period of time than if working at a heart rate of 164. Lactate threshold is roughly the pace and correlating average heart rate that can be held for approximately 1 hour when participating in a single sport such as cycling or running. Highly trained athletes can hold this pace for over an hour. Research has found that lactate threshold heart rate varies depending on the particular sport. Generally, running lactate threshold heart rates tend to be five to ten beats higher than cycling lactate threshold heart rates for an individual athlete.

Studies have shown lactate threshold to be a reliable predictor for endurance race performance, and the best news is that lactate threshold pace can be reduced through training. For example, if your current pace is 10 minutes per mile at your running lactate threshold, with the proper training you can decrease the pace (get faster) for the same heart rate and associated lactate level.

Training Zones

As I mentioned at the beginning of this chapter, scientists and coaches use different terms to explain energy production and lactate levels within the body. Table 3.1 cross-references some of the terms used by different coaches to explain energy production and training intensity levels. The same table also gives formulas to calculate training zones for cycling and running. Tables 3.2 and 3.3 are handy references that give you the training zones once you have determined your lactate threshold heart rate. The training zones utilized in this book are based on the work of Peter Janssen and further refined by triathlon endurance coach Joe Friel.

Zone 1

Zone 1 is used to build fitness in beginning athletes and is used for recovery purposes by more experienced athletes. The energy production is primarily aerobic. Zone 1 is also used in conjunction with Zone 2 to build exercise endurance for long distance racing.

Zone 2

Zone 2 is used to build base fitness and maintain current levels of fitness. Lactate level begins increasing, but the accumulation tends to be linear and can be managed by the body for very long periods of time in such

Table 3.2 Cycling Heart Rate Zones

Zone 1 Recovery	Zone 2 Aerobic	Zone 3 Tempo	Zone 4 Sub-threshold	Zone 5a Super-threshold	Zone 5b Aerobic Capacity	Zone 5c Anaerobic Capacity
90–108	109–122	123–128	129–136	137–140	141–145	146–150
91–109	110–123	124–129	130–137	138–141	142–146	147–151
91–109	110–124	125–130	131–138	139–142	143–147	148–152
92–110	111–125	126–130	131–139	140–143	144–147	148–153
92–111	112–125	126–131	132–140	141–144	145–148	149–154
93–112	113–126	127–132	133–141	142–145	146–149	150–155
94–112	113–127	128–133	134–142	143–145	146–150	151–156
94–113	114–128	129–134	135–143	144–147	148–151	152–157
95–114	115–129	130–135	136–144	145–148	149–152	153–158
96–115	116–130	131–136	137–145	146–149	150–154	155–159
97–116	117–131	132–137	138–146	147–150	151–155	156–161
97–117	118–132	133–138	139–147	148–151	152–156	157–162
98–118	119–133	134–139	140–148	149–152	153–157	158–163
98–119	120–134	135–140	141–149	150–153	154–158	159–164
99–120	121–134	135–141	142–150	151–154	155–159	160–165
100–121	122–135	136–142	143–151	152–155	156–160	161–166
100–122	123–136	137–142	143–152	153–156	157–161	162–167
101–123	124–137	138–143	144–153	154–157	158–162	163–168
101–124	125–138	139–144	145–154	155–158	159–163	164–169
102–125	126–138	139–145	146–155	156–159	160–164	165–170
103–126	127–140	141–146	147–156	157–160	161–165	166–171
104–127	128–141	142–147	148–157	158–161	162–167	168–173
104–128	129–142	143–148	149–158	159–162	163–168	169–174
105–129	130–143	144–148	149–159	160–163	164–169	170–175
106–129	130–143	144–150	151–160	161–164	165–170	171–176
106–130	131–144	145–151	152–161	162–165	166–171	172–177
107–131	132–145	146–152	153–162	163–166	167–172	173–178
107–132	133–146	147–153	154–163	164–167	168–173	174–179
108–133	134–147	148–154	155–164	165–168	169–174	175–180
109–134	135–148	149–154	155–165	166–169	170–175	176–181
109–135	136–149	150–155	156–166	167–170	171–176	177–182
110–136	137–150	151–156	157–167	168–171	172–177	178–183
111–137	138–151	152–157	158–168	169–172	173–178	179–185
112–138	139–151	152–158	159–169	170–173	174–179	180–186
112–139	140–152	153–160	161–170	171–174	175–180	181–187
113–140	141–153	154–160	161–171	172–175	176–181	182–188
113–141	142–154	155–161	162–172	173–176	177–182	183–189
114–142	143–155	156–162	163–173	174–177	178–183	184–190
115–143	144–156	157–163	164–174	175–178	179–184	185–191
115–144	145–157	158–164	165–175	176–179	180–185	186–192
116–145	146–158	159–165	166–176	177–180	181–186	187–193
116–146	147–159	160–166	167–177	178–181	182–187	188–194
117–147	148–160	161–166	167–178	179–182	183–188	189–195
118–148	149–160	161–167	168–179	180–183	184–190	191–197
119–149	150–161	162–168	169–180	181–184	185–191	192–198
119–150	151–162	163–170	171–181	182–185	186–192	193–199
120–151	152–163	164–171	172–182	183–186	187–193	194–200
121–152	153–164	165–172	173–183	184–187	188–194	195–201
121–153	154–165	166–172	173–184	185–188	189–195	196–202
122–154	155–166	167–173	174–185	186–189	190–196	197–203
122–155	156–167	168–174	175–186	187–190	191–197	198–204
123–156	157–168	169–175	176–187	188–191	192–198	199–205
124–157	158–169	170–176	177–188	189–192	193–199	200–206
124–158	159–170	171–177	178–189	190–193	194–200	201–207
125–159	160–170	171–178	179–190	191–194	195–201	202–208
125–160	161–171	172–178	179–191	192–195	196–202	203–209
126–161	162–172	173–179	180–192	193–196	197–203	204–210
127–162	163–173	174–180	181–193	194–197	198–204	205–211
127–163	164–174	175–181	182–194	195–198	199–205	206–212

Table 3.3 Running Heart Rate Zones

Zone 1 Recovery	Zone 2 Extensive Endurance	Zone 3 Intensive Endurance	Zone 4 Sub-threshold	Zone 5a Super-threshold	Zone 5b Anaerobic Endurance	Zone 5c Power
93–119	120–126	127–133	134–139	140–143	144–149	150–156
94–119	120–127	128–134	135–140	141–144	145–150	151–157
95–120	121–129	130–135	136–141	142–145	146–151	152–158
95–121	122–130	131–136	137–142	143–146	147–152	143–159
96–122	123–131	132–137	138–143	144–147	148–153	154–160
96–123	124–132	133–138	139–144	145–148	149–154	155–161
97–124	125–133	134–139	140–145	146–149	150–155	156–162
97–124	125–134	135–140	141–146	147–150	151–156	157–163
98–125	126–135	136–141	142–147	148–151	152–157	158–164
99–126	127–135	136–142	143–148	149–152	153–158	159–165
99–127	128–126	137–143	144–149	150–153	154–158	159–166
100–128	129–137	138–144	144–150	151–154	155–159	160–167
100–129	130–138	139–145	146–151	152–155	156–160	161–168
101–130	131–139	140–146	147–152	153–156	157–161	162–169
102–131	132–140	141–147	148–153	154–157	158–162	163–170
103–131	132–141	142–148	149–154	155–158	158–164	165–172
103–132	133–142	143–149	150–155	156–159	160–165	166–173
104–133	134–143	144–150	151–156	175–169	161–166	167–174
105–134	135–143	144–151	152–157	158–161	162–167	168–175
105–135	136–144	145–152	153–158	159–162	163–168	169–176
106–136	137–145	146–153	154–159	160–163	164–169	170–177
106–136	137–146	147–154	155–160	161–164	165–170	171–178
107–137	138–147	148–155	156–161	162–165	166–171	172–179
108–138	139–148	149–155	156–162	163–166	167–172	173–180
109–139	140–149	150–156	157–163	164–167	168–174	175–182
109–140	141–150	151–157	158–164	165–168	169–175	176–183
110–141	142–151	152–158	159–165	166–169	170–176	177–184
111–141	142–152	153–159	160–166	167–170	171–177	178–185
111–142	143–153	154–169	161–167	168–171	172–178	179–186
111–143	144–154	155–161	162–168	169–172	173–179	180–187
112–144	145–155	156–162	163–169	170–173	174–179	180–188
113–145	146–156	157–163	164–170	171–174	175–180	181–189
114–145	146–156	157–164	165–171	172–175	176–182	183–191
115–146	147–157	158–165	166–172	173–176	177–183	184–192
115–147	148–157	158–166	167–173	174–177	178–184	185–193
116–148	149–158	159–167	168–174	175–178	179–185	186–194
117–149	150–159	160–168	169–175	176–179	180–186	187–195
117–150	151–160	161–169	170–176	177–180	181–187	188–196
118–151	152–161	162–170	171–177	178–181	182–188	189–197
118–152	153–162	163–171	172–178	179–182	183–189	190–198
119–153	164–163	164–172	173–179	180–183	184–190	191–199
120–154	155–164	165–173	174–180	181–184	185–192	193–201
121–154	155–165	166–174	175–181	182–185	186–193	194–202
121–155	156–166	167–175	176–182	183–186	187–194	195–203
122–156	157–167	168–176	177–183	184–187	188–195	196–204
123–157	158–168	169–177	178–184	185–188	189–196	197–205
123–158	159–169	170–178	179–185	186–189	190–197	198–206
124–159	160–170	171–179	180–186	187–190	191–198	199–207
125–160	161–171	172–180	181–188	189–192	193–200	201–209
126–161	162–172	173–181	182–189	190–193	194–201	202–210
126–162	163–173	174–182	183–190	191–194	195–201	202–211
127–163	164–174	175–183	184–191	192–195	196–202	203–212
127–164	165–175	176–184	185–192	193–196	197–203	204–213
128–165	166–176	177–185	186–193	194–197	198–204	205–214
129–165	166–177	178–186	187–194	195–198	199–205	206–215
129–166	167–178	179–187	188–195	196–199	200–206	207–216
130–167	168–178	179–188	189–196	197–198	199–207	208–217
130–168	169–179	180–189	190–197	198–201	202–208	209–218
131–169	170–180	181–190	191–198	199–202	203–209	210–219
132–170	171–181	182–191	192–199	200–203	204–210	211–220

activities as Ironman distance training and racing. Within this intensity zone is what many coaches call "aerobic threshold." Some scientists and coaches define the lactate measurement of 2 mmol/L and the associated heart rate as aerobic threshold. There is disagreement about this value. (See Zone 5a for further discussion.)

Often Zones 1 and 2 are used in conjunction with drills to improve athletic skills. Good form improves athletic economy, which translates to less oxygen needed for a given pace.

Zone 3
Zone 3 intensity is used for early-season tempo work and to begin lactate threshold improvement. Zones 1 through 3 are used by experienced athletes training and racing in events lasting longer than about 3 hours.

Zone 4
This zone is used in conjunction with intervals, hill work, and steady-state work to improve lactate threshold speed and muscular endurance. It is common for the intervals in this zone to have a work-to-rest ratio of 3:1 or 4:1 in cycling and running.

Zone 5a
The lowest heart rate value in Zone 5a (100 percent of lactate threshold heart rate in Table 3.1) is called lactate threshold in this book. As previously mentioned, some coaches and scientists call this value "anaerobic threshold." Laboratories often associate a blood lactate value of 4 mmol/L with lactate threshold. Be aware that the 4mmol/L value is common for many athletes, but there are wide variations. Lactate threshold can be as low as 2 mmol/L or as high as 8 mmol/L for individual athletes. This is why the statement that "anaerobic threshold is 4 mmol/L" may be incorrect for some athletes. Quality laboratories typically provide lactate curves and interpret the data for you, eliminating a "one size fits all" value for both aerobic and lactate thresholds.

Zone 5a is used in conjunction with intervals, hill riding, and tempo rides to improve lactate threshold speed and muscular endurance. It is often used in conjunction with Zone 4.

Zone 5b

The major use for this zone is to improve anaerobic endurance. The cycling and running intervals in this zone often have a work-to-rest ratio of 1:1. This zone is also used in hill workouts.

Zone 5c

Zone 5c is fast, really fast, or powerful swimming, cycling, or running. For example, sprinting to the finish line or climbing hills out of the saddle elicits heart rates in this zone. Exercise in Zone 5c cannot be maintained for long periods of time. It is common for the intervals in this zone to have a work-to-rest ratio of 1:2 or more.

Estimating Heart Rate Training Zones

Often, beginning athletes do not own heart rate monitors nor do they have a desire to be tested at a laboratory. If you fit this description, your training zones are determined by rating of perceived exertion (RPE). You can use Table 3.1 as a guide. As a beginner, most of your training is accomplished in Zones 1 to 3.

If you have a low level of fitness and you're beginning an exercise program for the first time, it is best to have testing completed by your physician.

If you own a heart rate monitor and want to utilize it as a training tool, know there are various ways to estimate lactate threshold and the corresponding heart rate. An easy way to begin to use a heart rate monitor as a tool is to wear it and notice the heart rate values corresponding to the various RPE and breathing descriptions. Even if you have lactate threshold determined by laboratory testing, it is good practice to relate your RPE to heart rate values.

Laboratory testing typically includes a graded exercise component. In this test, the exercise workload increases incrementally and blood samples are taken at specific intervals to measure the level of lactate in the blood. Another laboratory method, also used during a graded exercise test, measures the ratio of oxygen to carbon dioxide being expelled from your respiratory system to estimate lactate threshold.

Finally, there are ways to estimate lactate threshold heart rate in the field. In order to get the best estimates, you need to be rested and highly motivated. If you do the test when you are tired, the results may be inaccurate. These tests, however, are not intended to find maximum heart rate. Ideally, you should build up some fitness prior to doing these tests. If you have been inactive for a long period of time, seek the advice of a physician first. For all of the tests, you need a wireless heart rate monitor, such as the models made by Polar, Timex, Nike, and many others. Selection of a heart rate monitor will depend on your goals and intended use.

Before beginning the tests to estimate lactate threshold heart rate, have a look at Table 3.1. It has a column entitled "RPE Borg Scale" and a column entitled "Breathing and Perception." The Borg Scale was originally designed to correlate with heart rate for young athletes, by adding zero to all the Borg numbers. For example, easy exercise at a perceived exertion value of 6 was intended to correlate to a heart rate of 60. Although the numbers do not always correlate exactly to heart rate, the RPE scale remains a valuable tool and is still widely used. For athletes training for their first triathlon, RPE and breathing can be used to estimate training zones, until high interest in triathlon warrants the purchase of a heart rate monitor.

The heart rate monitor is one tool available to estimate exercise intensity. Monitors come in a variety of models and price ranges. The least expensive models simply read heart rate. The more expensive models are capable of storing several hours' worth of data, which can then be downloaded into a computer for analysis.

The heart rate monitor system consists of a transmitter belt worn just below the breasts, strapped around the chest, together with a receiver worn on the wrist or mounted on the handlebar of the bike. The transmitter belt picks up electrical impulses from the heart and relays the information via an electromagnetic field to the receiver. The receiver then displays heart rate. It's like having a tachometer for the body.

Individual Time Trial

If lactate threshold pace, and the associated average heart rate, are roughly the pace that can be held for a 1- to 1.5-hour time trial, then it seems that the most straightforward way to find your personal lactate threshold heart rate is to assign yourself a 1-hour, all-out time trial. Ouch!

There are a few drawbacks to a 1-hour time trial that can cause inaccurate results, including:

Beginning athletes may not have the fitness to go all-out for 1 hour. Not only can this lead to inaccuracies, but it may endanger the safety and well-being of the athlete.

If a person has limited experience in sports, it is difficult to gauge what pace is all-out sustainable for an hour.

Maintaining focus and managing discomfort for an hour of all-out effort when you are alone (not in a race scenario) are challenging, even for the most experienced athletes.

Because of the drawbacks of a 1-hour time trial, a shorter time trial is more desirable.

Ten-minute Time Trial

After gaining some base fitness, you can conduct a short time trial to estimate your lactate threshold heart rate. Warm up for 10 to 15 minutes at RPE Zones 1 to 2. After the warm-up, you are going to run or ride for about 10 minutes, increasing your pace each minute. If you expect to go beyond the first minute, it is obvious you cannot sprint. As you increase pace, notice your heart rate at the end of each minute. How do you feel? What is your breathing rate?

There will be a point during your test when your breathing becomes noticeably labored and, some while later, a burning sensation begins to creep into your legs. Take note of your heart rate when you first feel your breathing become labored. For now, use this heart rate as your lactate threshold. Also take note of when you feel the burning sensation. That sensation can arise several minutes after your change in breathing. If you use the "burning leg" sensation to estimate lactate threshold heart rate, you might be overestimating your threshold. Overestimating your threshold will lead you to overestimate all the training zones, which means you might be working anaerobically when you intended to work aerobically. The result could be overtraining and underdevelopment of your aerobic system.

As you gain more sport experience, your estimated lactate threshold number can be further refined and improved. Also know that as an unfit novice endurance athlete gains fitness, the lactate threshold heart rate value increases. For very fit endurance athletes, the lactate threshold heart rate may not increase much with training, but the pace or speed at lactate threshold heart rate does improve, meaning that you will become faster at the same heart rate.

Race or Individual Time Trial of 20 to 30 Minutes

A "beginning triathlete" may not mean a "beginner" in endurance sports. Some athletes come to triathlon with experience in another sport such as running or cycling. Athletes with experience running 5k or 10k races can estimate lactate threshold heart rate from a race. Some athletes take 30 minutes to complete a 5k race, while others can run a distance of 10 kilometers in that time. For this reason, I use race completion time rather than distance to estimate lactate threshold heart rate.

If you are an experienced runner, you can use the average heart rate you achieve during a running race that takes between 20 and 30 minutes to estimate lactate threshold heart rate. This is best accomplished by using a heart rate monitor that calculates average heart rate over a selected interval or period.

The average heart rate you achieve in an all-out 20- or 30-minute race, with others running too, is higher than what you can produce in a 60- to 90-minute all-out race. For this reason, divide your 20- to 30-minute average race heart rate by 1.04. In other words, this value is about 104 percent of your lactate threshold heart rate.

For example, assume you run a 5k race and it takes you 25 minutes to finish. Your average heart rate produced during the race, excluding warm-up and cool-down heart rates, is 170 beats per minute. Your estimated lactate threshold heart rate is 170 divided by 1.04, or a value of 164.

Can you do your own 20-minute time trial, without going to a race? Yes. To conduct your own time trial, on the bike or running, find a flat course with no stoplights and minimal distractions. After a good warm-up, start your monitor and time trial as fast as possible for 20 minutes. This means metering your speed so you can produce the highest average, best effort for the full 20 minutes. (Avoid a fast 5-minute effort, then a slow fade.) Collect your heart rate average for the time trial and divide this value by 1.02. (You are dividing by 1.02 because the average heart rate that you produce in your own individual time trial is lower than the average heart rate you would produce in a race. Other racers can be very motivational!) For example, if your average heart rate for the 20-minute time trial is 160, then threshold heart rate can be estimated by dividing 160 by 1.02 to arrive at a value of 157.

The Zones

Now that you have an estimated lactate threshold heart rate, you can estimate training zones. You can calculate them yourself or use the charts provided in Tables 3.2 and 3.3 for cycling and running heart rate zones.

It is possible to use either your cycling or running threshold and then use that value to estimate the threshold heart rate for the other sport. A good rule of thumb for multisport athletes is that running lactate threshold (LT) is often five to ten beats higher than cycling LT. For example, if you have a running LT heart rate of 164, a reasonable start is to estimate cycling LT at 154.

Can lactate threshold heart rates and training zones change? Yes. Does everyone follow the five- to ten-beat rule of thumb to calculate the difference between cycling and running LT? Most of the time, yes. There are, however, exceptions. As you gain experience using the numbers, partnered with RPE, if your sport training zones seem off, you can hone in on a more precise number by completing an LT test in each sport. Continuously verify the accuracy of the values by taking note of your heart rates during training and racing.

In this book, heart rate is one tool used, in conjunction with RPE, to quantify training and racing intensities for cycling and running. As you gain more fitness and experience racing, at some point you may want to get faster. When it becomes important to you to achieve a personal best performance, pace at a given heart rate becomes more critical to your training. Heart rate and specific pace training is not included in this book for beginners.

Other tools for determining workloads on the bike are power readings produced by CompuTrainer, Power-Tap, and Polar, SRM, and Ergomo instruments. It is good to know there are tools available to further your technical training; however, instructions on how to use those tools are not included in this book.

For swimming you can use a test time trial to establish baseline fitness. Not all training plans in this book include the test. This is because for beginners, the baseline test may require more endurance prior to completing the test.

Once you have base endurance and test results, you can use your average pace in conjunction with a pace clock and RPE as tools for swimming intensity.

Swim Time Trial

Testing for swim pace is done after swimming endurance has been built. Improving T1-Pace over several weeks and months of training is a marker of improved fitness and certainly a goal to shoot for. To find your T1-Pace, after a warm-up of 10 to 20 minutes, complete the time trial for the appropriate distance race.

Sprint Distance

Swim 3 x 100 with 20 seconds' rest between each one. The goal of the set is to swim at the highest possible sustained speed to achieve the lowest average time. In other words, do not swim the first 100 fast and be 15 seconds slower on the third 100. Watch the clock and get your time on each 100. Average the time for all three 100s to establish a T1-Pace.

For example, a reasonable swim might look like 1:25, 1:21, and 1:24; so the T1-Pace would be 1:23. One would *not* want to swim 1:20, 1:25, and 1:35—a 15-second difference between the first and third 100. It is best if all three 100s are within 5 seconds of one another.

Olympic or Ironman Distance Triathlon

Swim 3 x 300 with 30 seconds' rest between each one. As with the 100s in the sprint distance test, the goal of the set is to swim at the highest average speed possible. An accurate test is when all three 300s are within 15 seconds of each other. In other words, do not swim a fast, first 300 and have the third 300 be 20 seconds slower.

Watch the clock and get your time on each 300. Average the time for all three 300s and divide the average by three to establish a T1-Pace, for a 100-yard distance. For example, if you swam a 3:30, 3:25, and 3:22, the average time for the 300s is 3:27. Divide that result by three to obtain a T1-Pace of 1:09.

Practical Application

If you are a beginning endurance athlete, as you gain more fitness your lactate threshold heart rate will probably change. More than likely, it will increase. As you move toward a rating of "high fitness," your threshold heart rate tends to stabilize. But you can further improve your speed at lactate threshold. Earlier in the chapter, I mentioned that lactate threshold is highly trainable: This is what I meant.

While a heart rate monitor is an excellent tool and provides an estimate of metabolic processes occurring within the body, it is important to understand factors that affect heart rate values. Some of these factors are heat, humidity, altitude, hydration status and nutrition status, approaching illness, quality of recent sleep, lifestyle stress, and inadequate recovery from previous workouts, to name only a few. These factors can drive heart rate values higher or lower than what seems "normal" to you for any given pace. Also, outside interference from electrical lines and other athletes' heart rate monitors can cause erroneous readings. Some heart rate monitor manufacturers have "coded" transmitter belts and receivers. This coding reduces erroneous readings from the previously mentioned sources. It is important that you learn to interpret the heart rate values displayed on your monitor.

It is also important to know that when a training zone range is assigned on one of the training plans within this book, such as "easy run in Zones 1 and 2" it is *not* your goal to maximize training time at the top end of the assigned zone. Learn to listen to your body and lower the intensity when your body is telling you it's tired or stressed. On the days when you feel full of energy, it's okay to spend more time at the high end of the assigned training zone. Develop and use good judgment in your training. It is key to your long-term success.

References

Bernhardt, Gale. *The Female Cyclist: Gearing up a Level.* Boulder, CO: VeloPress, 1999.

————. *Training Plans for Multisport Athletes.* Boulder, CO: VeloPress, 2000: 3–16.

Burke, Edmund R., Ph.D. *Serious Cycling.* Champaign, IL: Human Kinetics, 1995.

Edwards, Sally. *The Heart Rate Monitor Book.* 2nd ed. Boulder, CO: VeloPress, 2002.

Friel, Joe. *The Cyclist's Training Bible: A Complete Training Guide for the Competitive Road Cyclist.* 3rd ed. Boulder, CO: VeloPress, 2003.

————. *The Triathlete's Training Bible: A Complete Training Guide for the Competitive Multisport Athlete.* 2nd ed. Boulder, CO: VeloPress, 2003.

Hart, Corey. Colorado State University Human Performance Lab, USA Cycling Expert Coach, personal testing and interview, February 25 and March 10, 2003.

Janssen, Peter G. J. M., M.D. *Training Lactate Pulse-Rate.* Polar Electro Oy, 1987.

————. *Lactate Threshold Training.* Champaign, IL: Human Kinetics, 2001: 98, 107, 109.

Martin, David E., Ph.D., and Peter N. Coe. *Better Training for Distance Runners.* 2nd ed. Champaign, IL: Human Kinetics, 1997: 99, 101.

McArdle, William D., et al. *Exercise Physiology: Energy, Nutrition, and Human Performance.* 5th ed. Philadelphia: Lippincott Williams & Wilkins, 1991.

Shepard, Roy J., and Per-Olof Astrand. *Endurance in Sport: Olympic Encyclopaedia of Sports Medicine,* vol. 2. Malden, MA: Blackwell Science Ltd., 2000: 314–22.

Chapter 4

Unfit Beginner
Plan for a Sprint Distance Triathlon

*Ordinary people, even weak people, can do extraordinary things
through temporary courage generated by a situation. But the person of character
does not need the situation to generate his courage. It is a part of his being and a
standard approach to all life's challenges.*
—Michael S. Josephson, Founder and CEO, Josephson Institute of Ethics

This training plan is designed for a beginning triathlete, someone who
needs an effective plan with minimal time commitment. The plan builds
overall fitness, along with the triathlon-specific endurance needed to comfortably complete a sprint distance event. You just need a place to begin ...

Goal
Complete a sprint distance triathlon at the end of 12 weeks of preparation. Race distance is approximately 450 yards of swimming, a 15-mile
bike ride, and a 3.1-mile run.

Profile

You are a beginning triathlete more concerned with comfortably completing a triathlon than with setting any new speed records. Your schedule allows training 30 to 45 minutes on weekdays, and one of the weekend days permits longer training, up to 2 hours. Optimizing training time is essential: You need 2 days off each week for other lifestyle activities.

Before beginning Week 1 of the plan displayed in Table 4.1, you are capable of swimming 50 yards without stopping, cycling 30 minutes three times per week, and, although you have trained as a runner in the past, you are not running currently. (See table at the end of this chapter.)

If you happen to have more endurance than described in the preceding paragraph, you can consider beginning the plan in Week 4. Athletes beginning in Week 4 are already capable of swimming eight repeats of 75 yard or meters or 8 x 75, resting 30 seconds between each 75. These athletes also have the cycling endurance to ride twice per week for around 30 minutes and to ride a third day for an hour. They can run comfortably for 15 to 30 minutes, twice per week.

The Plan

The plan in Table 4.1 has a general pattern of a day off on Monday, a swim on Tuesday, a combination (combo) or "brick" workout on Wednesday, a swim on Thursday, a combination or brick workout on Friday, a long bike ride on Saturday, and Sunday is a day off. (A bike/run workout is typically called a "brick" in multisport lingo.) If you need a different schedule, you can move the workouts around. General guidelines for this plan include keeping similar workouts 48 hours apart and trying to avoid "stacking" missed workouts.

For example, it might work better for you to swim on Monday and have Tuesday as your day off. It might also work better for you to have Friday as your day off and to complete your combination or brick on Saturday and your long ride on Sunday. Switching workout days to accommodate your overall schedule or just to make changes for 1 week is fine. It is not good, however, to stack workouts.

What is "stacking workouts"? Stacking is what occurs when an athlete misses one or more workouts early in the week, then tries to make up for lost time on the weekend. A stacker is a close relative of the weekend warrior. For example, the stacker completes the swim on Tuesday, but takes Monday, Wednesday, Thursday, and Friday as athletic days off—meanwhile life and business are full throttle on those days. Stackers believe they can make up for lost time by doing all the work within 2 days. They complete a swim and a combo workout on Saturday, then a long bike and a second combo workout or brick on Sunday. Packing all or most of the work into 2 days is a nice invitation for illness or injury.

This plan does not assign specific days for strength training. The reason no strength training is specified is that many beginning triathletes need a plan that minimizes workout time. If you have the time and desire to strength train, you can add a weight routine on the days off or after any of the aerobic workouts. A suggestion for a manageable routine is to complete two or three sets of twelve to fifteen repetitions of the following: leg press, lat pull-down, chest press, seated row, abdominal exercises, and back extension exercises. Refer to Chapter 12 for more ideas on strength training.

For all the workouts in the plan, use RPE to judge intensity and speed. This RPE is referred to by "Zone." Find a reference scale for RPE and the related zone in Chapter 3. If you have a heart rate monitor and know your training zones, you can use it as well. Heart rate monitor or not, all athletes will find it valuable to develop their RPE.

Weeks 1–4

Swim

In most weeks, the swim workout on Thursday is a repeat of Tuesday, with the exception of a change in intensity. For Weeks 1 to 4, the goal on Thursday is to put less effort into the swim than on Tuesday. Keep all swimming intensity in Weeks 1 to 4 in Zones 1 to 2. Try to relax when you swim, getting the most distance out of each stroke, with the least amount of effort. The time budgeted in the plan is 30 minutes per swim workout. You may or may not need 30 minutes. Experienced swimmers may want to add some additional warm-up or cool-down swimming. Each swim workout is numbered.

Workout 1: This plan assumes you can swim down and back (50 yards or meters) in a standard pool. Although the measure "yards" is used in each description, yards and meters are interchangeable. The first workout simply requires swimming 10 x 50 yards, resting about 45 seconds (45 sec. RI) between each 50 yards. You may have to rest an entire minute between each 50, and that is okay. If you do not use a specific warm-up or cooldown, make the first and last couple of 50s very easy.

Workout 2: Swim 10 x 50 yards, resting 30 to 45 seconds between each 50 yards.

Workout 3: Swim 10 x 50 yards, resting 20 to 30 seconds between each 50 yards.

Workout 4: Bump the distance up a bit to 8 x 75 yards, resting 30 seconds between each 75 yards. By now, you are building some endurance in the pool. If you would like to swim a bit longer, add a few yards of warm-up before the 8 x 75 and/or add a few yards after the main set. In the weeks to come, you can add warm-up, cooldown, and a few yards of kicking to any day on which you have the time and energy to do so.

Combination Days

In Weeks 1 to 4, to optimize training time and build endurance in cycling and running, you run and walk first. Immediately following the run/walk, hop on a bike and ride for a "combo" workout. Later in the plan, there are bike rides immediately followed by a run, or a "brick." RPE for all combo workouts is in Zones 1 to 2 for Weeks 1 to 4.

The combination format is perfect for the time-crunched athlete, and the workouts can be done easily at a club or at home, inside or outside. Indoors, running and walking can be done on a treadmill and cycling on a stationary bicycle or trainer. Outdoor workouts can be accomplished from your home or car (mobile transition area). For the first 4 weeks of the plan, running and walking are first, then cycling. This format is to minimize injury risk and build endurance. The format changes some as the plan progresses.

Let's look at one specific workout—Wednesday in Week 1 of the plan. Begin the workout by running for 1 minute, then walking for 1 minute. Repeat this sequence of running and walking five times. Immediately following the last walk segment, hop on a bike and ride for 30 minutes. The plan shows a total workout time of 40 minutes. If you have the time, fitness, and desire, riding longer, up to 45 minutes, is fine. I would recommend wearing cycling shorts for both segments to maximize comfort and minimize clothes changing. Some people prefer wearing running shorts for both workouts and that works as well—but is less comfortable.

The plan for Weeks 1 to 4 shows run time increasing and total run/walk time building. Thursday of Week 4, the walking is removed. Although no more walking is specifically outlined in the plan past Week 4, you can continue a run/walk pattern on your own.

Long Bike
On Saturday of Weeks 1 to 3, bike for 45 minutes nonstop. In Week 4, ride only 30 minutes. Keep all the rides on a mostly flat course and RPE in Zones 1 to 2. As the plan progresses, the long ride builds to around 2 hours.

Weeks 5–8

Swim
In Weeks 5 and 6, the swim workout on Thursday is a repeat of Tuesday. Your goal on Thursday is to put less effort into the swim than on Tuesday. Keep all swimming intensity in Weeks 5 and 6 in Zones 1 to 2. The specific workouts described for Weeks 5 through 8 are the bare minimum. In all cases, you can do additional swimming, including warm-up, cooldown, drills, or kicking up, to 30 minutes—if you have the time and energy. Each swim workout is numbered.

Workout 5: Swim 8 x 75 yards, resting 20 seconds between each 75-yard swim.

Workout 6:   Swim 8 x 75 yards, resting 10 seconds between each
75-yard swim.
For Weeks 7 and 8, the swim intensity on Tuesday is
Zones 1 to 3 and the intensity on Thursday is Zones 1 to 2.

Workout 7:   Swim 5 x 100 yards, resting 20 seconds between each
100-yard swim.

Workout 8:   Swim 5 x 100 yards, resting 10 seconds between each
100-yard swim.

Combination Days

In Weeks 1 to 4, you used combo workouts to build running endurance.
Those combo workouts included running, walking, and cycling. In
Weeks 5 to 8, the walking segments are no longer necessary because you
have built running endurance. You may want to continue utilizing a
run/walk format on your own, and that works, too.

For Weeks 5 through 8, Tuesday remains a combo workout—meaning you run, immediately following that with a bike ride. In Weeks 5, 6,
and 7, keep the run segment on combo days in Zones 1 and 2. The bike
segment on these days is in Zones 1 to 3. If you are feeling fresh and
frisky, include more Zone 3 intensity. If there is minimal zip in your doo-
dah, keep the intensity mostly in the lower zones. In Week 8, keep both
sports in Zones 1 and 2.

Bricks

For years, the term "brick" has been used to describe a bike ride, immediately followed by a run. While some believe the term has a negative
connotation for how your legs feel when running just after a bike ride,
I'd rather think of bricks as good foundation blocks for race day.

The plan shows 45-minute bricks on Friday of Weeks 5 through 7 and
a 30-minute brick on Friday of Week 8. In all cases, keep your overall
RPE in Zones 1 to 2 and include three to six times of 20- to 30-second
(sec.) accelerations (accels) in both sports. After each acceleration, take
at least 2 minutes at RPE Zone 1 to recover. To accelerate means to gently increase your speed. Accels are not all-out, explosive sprints.

Long Bike
On Saturdays, cycling endurance builds from 1 hour in Week 5 to 1.5 hours in Week 7. These rides can be on a rolling course at RPE in Zones 1 to 2.

Option 2, Week 8

Notice that Week 8 is a rest week. This means training volume is reduced to allow for recovery and adaptation. Week 8, shown in Table 4.1, continues the pattern of training used in Weeks 5 through 7. A second option for Week 8 changes the pattern a bit and offers a race day dress rehearsal on Sunday, which helps some athletes feel more prepared on race day.

In Option 2, the Monday, Tuesday, and Wednesday workouts remain the same as shown in Table 4.1. The change is to make Thursday and Saturday days off. Friday is an easy bike ride in Zones 1 and 2. Sunday is a race simulation day, with reduced distances for the bike and the run. For the simulation, plan to take all your gear to the swimming pool. Begin by swimming 500 yards in the pool, then transition to a 30-minute bike ride. After the bike ride, transition to a 15-minute run. Keep the RPE of all sports mostly in Zones 1 to 2. To experience feeling light and fast, you can include a few 20- to 30-second accelerations in each sport.

Weeks 9–12

Swim
In all remaining weeks, make the main set of the Tuesday swim in Zones 1 to 3 and the Thursday swim in Zones 1 to 2. Include warm-up yards before the main set and cool down with at least 100 yards of easy swimming afterward. If you have time and energy, it is fine to add a few yards after the main set and before cooldown, swimming up to 30 minutes total.

> **Workout 9:** After a few minutes of warm-up in the pool, swim 500 yards nonstop and take note of your time. As you continue your triathlon journey past this first race, your 500 time should improve with training. If your race is in open water, try to get to a swim beach with a lifeguard

for your Thursday workout. Inform the lifeguard you are practicing for your first triathlon and ask him or her to keep an eye on you. Swim about the same amount of time in open water that you have in your previous workouts. Feel free to relax and take your time. If possible, swim to a buoy that is around 25 yards out, then swim back. Rest as much as you need between each "outing." If you are not swimming in open water on race day or do not have access to a safe open-water swimming situation, the swim workout on Thursday is a repeat of Tuesday.

Workout 10: After warming up with a few yards at the pool on Tuesday, swim 3 x 200 yards, resting 15 seconds between each 200. In total, swim up to 30 minutes. On Thursday, swim about 15 to 30 minutes in open water or repeat the Tuesday workout.

Workout 11: After the warm-up, swim 500 yards nonstop at the pool. Make the odd-numbered 25-yard segments very easy and the even-numbered 25-yard segments faster. For Thursday, repeat the Tuesday workout or swim up to 30 minutes in open water.

Workout 12: After a good warm-up at the pool, swim 500 yards nonstop. Make the first 100 yards of your swim very easy. On the second 100, try to relax your arms on the out-of-water portion (recovery). For the third 100 yards, focus on a strong hand pull. On the fourth 100 yards, use a strong underwater pull and relaxed recovery. Finally, make each 25-yard length a bit faster on the final 100 yards. This is the same strategy to use during the swim on race day. On Thursday after a short warm-up, swim 250 yards at race pace. Include four accelerations consisting of twelve powerful arm strokes during the swim, whenever the mood strikes you. These short accelerations in speed, with long recoveries, are known as "speed play" or fartlek intervals. Take at least twenty-four strokes of easy swimming to recover after each one. After a short cooldown, get out of the pool. A second option for Thursday is to take the day off, which won't hurt you a bit and may help on race day.

Bricks

In Weeks 5 to 8, the brick workout was on Friday and was an easy workout with only a few accelerations or speed pickups. In Weeks 9 to 12, complete the brick on Wednesday and include some longer accelerations in the run segment. For example, on Wednesday of Week 9, bike for 20 minutes in Zones 1 and 2. Transition to a run that includes 1-minute accelerations. At the end of each acceleration, RPE should be Zone 3 or 4. After a very easy 1-minute jog, complete another acceleration. Repeat this pattern five times. After the accelerations, finish your run in Zone 1.

All the brick workouts follow the pattern described in the last paragraph. The entire bike ride is in Zones 1 and 2. The run begins in Zones 1 to 2 and includes accelerations into Zone 3 or 4. Do not try sprinting in an all-out effort during the acceleration time.

Combination Days

For the combination workouts in Weeks 9 to 12, complete a run, immediately followed by a bike ride. Both workouts are in Zones 1 and 2.

Long Bike

On Saturdays, cycling endurance builds to between 1.5 and 2 hours. The long ride is where overall race endurance is developed. The long ride can be on a rolling course and RPE is anywhere in Zones 1 to 3, which is the intensity of your entire race.

If you have not been carrying water or an energy drink on bike rides lasting more than an hour, it's time to begin. The very best sports drink is the one that tastes good to you. If your best friend drinks Brand-X and you think it tastes like duck-pond water, find an alternative. A rule of thumb is to consume 150 to 250 calories of carbohydrates per hour for workouts and races under 3 hours. (See Chapter 14 for more detail on nutrition.) Practice drinking every 15 minutes. This general guideline is for training as well as the race. If you decide to carry water instead of a sports drink, supplement the water with a sports bar made up of mostly carbohydrate calories. The bar or drink can contain some protein, but keep fat to a minimum.

Race Week

In the final weeks prior to the race, try to drive the course at least once. This is often done the day before the race if you live a good distance from the race venue. If you happen to live close to the course, consider doing some portion of a workout on part of the course.

In the final days leading up to race morning, refrain from doing more than is shown on the schedule. Certainly do not do a test event the day before the triathlon, just to be sure you can "make it." This behavior is the sure mark of a beginner and will leave you tired for the race itself, which is no fun.

Fun is the most important goal for race day. Try to relax and enjoy your fitness. Begin each event within the race slightly slower than you plan to finish it. A good plan is to begin each segment of the event in Zones 1 to 2 and finish in Zone 3. Try to keep the pace in the range you experienced in training. The mission—should you choose to accept it— is to finish the event with a smile on your face. With the mission accomplished, who knows what your multisport future may hold?

Table 4.1 Unfit Beginner Plan for a Sprint Distance Triathlon

Week	Monday	Tuesday	Wednesday	Thursday
1	Day off	Workout 1 Swim 10 x 50 (45 sec. RI) Zones 1–2	Combo (Run 1 min., walk 1 min.) x 5 Bike 30 min. Total time 40 min. Zones 1–2	Workout 1 Swim 10 x 50 (45 sec. RI) Zone 1
2	Day off	Workout 2 Swim 10 x 50 (30–45 sec. RI) Zones 1–2	Combo (Run 2 min., walk 1 min.) x 5 Bike 30 min. Total time 45 min. Zones 1–2	Workout 2 Swim 10 x 50 (30–45 sec. RI) Zone 1
3	Day off	Workout 3 Swim 10 x 50 (20–30 sec. RI) Zones 1–2	Combo (Run 3 min., walk 1 min.) x 5 Bike 30 min. Total time 50 min. Zones 1–2	Workout 3 Swim 10 x 50 (20–30 sec. RI) Zone 1
4	Day off	Workout 4 Swim 8 x 75 (30 sec. RI) Zones 1–2	Combo (Run 5 min., walk 1 min.) x 3 Bike 30 min. Total time 48 min. Zones 1–2	Workout 4 Swim 8 x 75 (30 sec. RI) Zone 1
5	Day off	Workout 5 Swim 8 x 75 (20 sec. RI) Zones 1–2	Combo Run 15 min. Zones 1–2 Bike 30 min. Zones 1–3	Workout 5 Swim 8 x 75 (20 sec. RI) Zone 1
6	Day off	Workout 6 Swim 8 x 75 (10 sec. RI) Zones 1–2	Combo Run 20 min. Zones 1–2 Bike 25 min. Zones 1–3	Workout 6 Swim 8 x 75 (10 sec. RI) Zone 1
7	Day off	Workout 7 Swim 5 x 100 (20 sec. RI) Zones 1–3	Combo Run 25 min. Zones 1–2 Bike 20 min. Zones 1–3	Workout 7 Swim 5 x 100 (20 sec. RI) Zones 1–2
8	Day off	Workout 8 Swim 5 x 100 (10 sec. RI) Zones 1–3	Combo Run 15 min. Bike 15 min. Zones 1–2	Workout 8 Swim 5 x 100 (10 sec. RI) Zones 1–2
9	Day off	Workout 9 Swim 500 nonstop Zones 1–3	BRICK Bike 20 min. Run 25 min., with 5 x (1-min. accel, 1 min. EZ)	Workout 9 Swim 500 nonstop Zones 1–2
10	Day off	Workout 10 Swim 3 x 200 (15 sec. RI) Zones 1–3	BRICK Bike 15 min. Run 30 min., with 6–8 x (1-min. accel, 1 min. EZ)	Workout 10 Swim 15–30 min. steady or repeat Tuesday Zones 1–2
11	Day off	Workout 11 Swim 500 nonstop Zones 1–3	BRICK Bike 20 min. Run 25 min., with 6–8 x (1-min. accel, 1 min. EZ)	Workout 11 Swim 500 nonstop Zones 1–2
12	Day off	Workout 12 Swim 400–500 nonstop Zones 1–3	BRICK Bike 20 min. Run 10 min., with a few 20-sec. accels in both sports	Workout 12 Swim 250 nonstop or take the day off

Friday	Saturday	Sunday	Weekly Totals
Combo (**Run** 1 min., walk 1 min.) x 7–8 **Bike** 30 min. Total time 45 min. Zones 1–2	**Bike** 45 min. Zones 1–2	Day off	3 hr., 15 min.
Combo (**Run** 2 min., walk 1 min.) x 5–7 **Bike** 30 min. Total time 45 min. Zones 1–2	**Bike** 45 min. Zones 1–2	Day off	3 hr., 15 min.
Combo (**Run** 4 min., walk 1 min.) x 5 **Bike** 30 min. Total time 55 min. Zones 1–2	**Bike** 45 min. Zones 1–2	Day off	3 hr., 15 min.
Combo **Run** 15 min. **Bike** 30 min. Total time 45 min. Zones 1–2	**Bike** 30 min. Zones 1–2	Day off	2 hr., 45 min.
BRICK **Bike** 30 min. **Run** 15 min. Zones 1–2, with 30-sec. accels	**Bike** 1 hr. Zones 1–2	Day off	3 hr., 30 min.
BRICK **Bike** 30 min. **Run** 15 min. Zones 1–2, with 30-sec. accels	**Bike** 1 hr., 15 min. Zones 1–2	Day off	3 hr., 45 min.
BRICK **Bike** 25 min. **Run** 20 min. Zones 1–2, with 30-sec. accels	**Bike** 1 hr., 30 min. Zones 1–2	Day off	4 hr.
BRICK **Bike** 15 min. **Run** 15 min. Zones 1–2, with 30-sec. accels	**Bike** 1 hr. Zones 1–2	Day off	3 hr., 15 min.
Combo **Run** 15 min. **Bike** 30 min. Zones 1–2	**Bike** 1 hr., 30 min. Zones 1–3	Day off	4 hr.
Combo **Run** 15 min. **Bike** 30 min. Zones 1–2	**Bike** 1 hr., 30 min. to 1 hr., 45 min. Zones 1–3	Day off	4 hr., 15 min.
Swim 500 nonstop Zones 1–2	**Bike** 1 hr., 30 min. to 2 hr. Zones 1–3	Day off	4 hr., 30 min.
Day off	**BRICK** **Bike** 20 min. **Run** 10 min., with a few accels in both sports	Race!	1 hr., 30 min. + race time

Chapter 5

Fit Beginner
Plan for a Sprint Distance Triathlon

Opportunity knocks; temptation knocks the door down.
—Anonymous

If you are currently fit, doing some type of aerobic work three to four times per week, and looking to complete your first sprint distance event, this plan is for you. Your current aerobic fitness can come from any source, such as spin classes, aerobics class, step aerobics, inline skating, bicycling outdoors, or similar activities. You may or may not be strength training prior to beginning the plan.

Goal

Complete a sprint distance triathlon at the end of 12 weeks of preparation. Race distance is approximately 450 yards of swimming, a 15-mile bike ride, and a 3.1-mile run.

Profile

Although you are currently fit, you are a beginning triathlete. Your main interest is in completing a triathlon comfortably. The triathlon can be an organized event, or you can use this plan to complete your own self-designed event. Your schedule allows for training 30 to 45 minutes on weekdays, with longer training on one of the weekend days, up to 2 hours.

Before beginning Week 1 of the plan displayed in Table 5.1, you are capable of swimming 50 yards without stopping, cycling 30 minutes twice per week, and you can comfortably run 10 to 20 minutes. (See table at the end of this chapter.)

If you happen to have more endurance than described in the last paragraph, you can consider beginning the plan in Week 4 or Week 7. If you begin the training deeper into the plan, the first week of training you aim for should look easy to accomplish.

The Plan

The plan in Table 5.1 has a general pattern of a strength-training day or a day off on Monday. Tuesday is a run, Wednesday and Friday are swims, Thursday is a bike ride, Saturday is a run or a brick (a bike ride, immediately followed by a run), and Sunday is the long ride day or a day off.

If it works better for you to move the workouts around, you can do this. Try to keep similar workouts 48 hours apart. In other words, it is preferable to swim on Tuesday and Thursday instead of Tuesday and Wednesday. It may better fit your schedule to combine two of the workouts on one day so you can have 1 or 2 days totally off from scheduled exercise. For example, you might like to swim and run on Tuesday, take Wednesday off, swim and bike on Thursday, and take Friday off. Be careful about "stacking" workouts. (See Chapter 4 for a description of stacking.)

If you are currently strength training, you can keep your current routine. Be aware and notice if strength training is taking too much energy away from your swimming, cycling, and running. If this is the case, consider reducing the exercises, sets, or repetitions to allow higher-quality workouts during the aerobic sessions. Another option for strength training is to use the routine listed in Chapter 12.

For all the workouts in the plan, you can use RPE or heart rate to judge intensity and speed. Your intensity gauge is referred to by "zone." An intensity reference scale for RPE and the related zone is in Chapter 3. With or without a heart rate monitor, it is valuable for all athletes to develop their RPE.

Swim

The plan shows a minimum amount of swimming to help you complete the event successfully. If you come from a swimming background, you may want to add more warm-up or cool-down yards to what is shown in Table 5.1. The general strategy of the plan is to begin by swimming 50-yard (or 50-meter) repeats, with generous rest, totaling 500 yards. Most standard pools are either 25 yards or 25 meters long. Ask the lifeguard how long your pool is if you are not sure. As the plan progresses, the length of your swims increases and rest decreases. You are building endurance.

For example, on Wednesday of Week 1, swim ten repeats of 50 yards, taking a 45-second rest interval (45 sec. RI) between each swim. The swim should feel easy, Zone 1 intensity. By Wednesday of Week 3, you swim ten repeats of 50 yards, taking only 10 seconds of rest between each swim.

In Weeks 4 through 6, you can increase the intensity some from Zone 1 to 2. This is a subtle increase in speed. As you increase speed, try to relax. On the Friday workouts during this time, build the distance of your swim to 75 and then 100 yards, without stopping. Aim for 20-second rest intervals (20 sec. RI) during these workouts. If you find you are having trouble holding the rest interval, try to relax and not swim so hard. The Wednesday swim in Week 6 is 200 yards steady (yahoo!). Take 1 minute of rest, then complete ten repeats of 25 yards, with 15-second rest intervals between each one. The odd-numbered swims (1, 3, 5, 7, and 9) should be very relaxed and easy swimming; the even-numbered swims (2, 4, 6, 8, and 10) should remain relaxed, but should be faster than the odds.

For Weeks 7 through 9, you will complete the Wednesday swims at intensity Zones 1 through 3. In general, begin with Zone 1 and finish the set with Zone 3. Learning to meter intensity is key to competing successfully in the triathlon. The last thing you want to do is go out too fast and "blow up" at the end of the swim, struggling to complete the distance. The intensity levels of Friday swims during this time are in Zones 1 to 2.

Your goal will not always be to shoot for the highest intensity. The logic that some workouts need to be easy so that you can get faster may seem counterintuitive. However, this strategy is critical for all levels of successful athletes.

In Week 10, the Wednesday swim changes so that you swim two easy 50s, then two fast 50s, keeping intensity within Zones 1 and 2. You will have generous 30-second rest intervals to help you keep your swimming form intact. On Friday of Week 10, you have your first 500-yard swim, the approximate distance of your race. Begin the swim in Zone 1 and finish in Zone 3. Beginning at a pace easier and slower than you think is possible, and finishing faster than you began is called "negative-split." Most world records are set using a negative-split strategy.

After you complete your 500-yard swims on Friday of Weeks 10 and 12, there are optional 50-yard repeats. Complete these swims only if you have the time and energy.

Bike

The Thursday bike rides shown in the plan are all 30 minutes long and to be completed at Zones 1 to 2 intensity. The goal of the Thursday rides is to work on good pedaling technique in order to improve economy. In short, improving economy gives you more speed for a given effort level. There are three workouts designed to improve your pedaling economy:

Spin-ups: After a warm-up, gently increase your cadence over the course of 30 seconds or so. "Cadence" refers to the number of times one of your legs completes one revolution of pedaling. You can count the number of times your right (or left) leg is at the bottom of the pedal stroke over the course of 15 seconds and multiply that value by four to get revolutions per minute. Inexperienced cyclists tend to have a low cadence, 50 revolutions per minute (rpm), while experienced cyclists have a higher cadence, 80 rpm or more, on a flat course. When your butt begins bouncing off your bicycle seat, reduce your cadence and recover a minute or two before beginning the next spin-up. Complete four to six spin-ups. Be sure to spin easy at the end of the workout.

Isolated leg training (ILT): Isolated leg training improves pedaling technique as you apply force around as much of the pedal stroke as possible. If you are indoors on a wind trainer, you can place a chair on either side of your bicycle to rest one leg while the other leg is working. If you are on the road, simply relax one leg while the other one does the majority of the work. After a warm-up, pedal with one leg for 30 seconds. At the top of the pedal stroke, drive your knee and toes forward. As your foot begins the downward motion, apply pressure to the pedal as if you were scraping mud off your foot on the curb of a street. As your foot moves to the back of the pedal stroke, lift and unweight your foot and prepare to drive your knee and toes forward again. If you have a "dead spot" in your pedal stroke, it becomes obvious immediately during this drill. Think of your foot and leg as the lever mechanism powering an old-style locomotive. You want that lever constantly delivering power to the wheel. When you finish working one leg, switch to the other leg for 30 seconds. After completing one cycle with each leg, spin with both legs for 30 to 60 seconds. Be sure to end the session by spinning easy with both legs.

90 rpm: Pedal the entire session at a cadence of 90 revolutions per minute (rpm) or more. If you are unable to pedal at 90, rest for a while and begin again. You are either pedaling at 90 rpm or higher, or you are resting. If you don't have a cadence sensor as part of your bicycle computer, you can count the number of times your right leg reaches the bottom of the pedal stroke in

15 seconds. The number should be 22 or higher.
On Sunday bike rides, you will build endurance for the
bicycle portion of the event and for the entire event.
Your Sunday rides begin at Zone 1 intensity for 30 min-
utes and build to a long ride of 2 hours in Zones 1 to 3.
This is the same intensity and speed to use on race day.

In Weeks 7, 8, and 10, try to ride a course that is similar to the course you will ride on race day. If you have been training on pancake-flat courses, you will have an unwelcome surprise on race day when you find the course is hilly. Know what the course demands, then train on actual parts of the course or on a course with similar terrain.

For every ride longer than an hour, carry some type of sports drink. A good rule of thumb for races less than 3 hours long is to consume approximately 16 to 24 ounces of fluid and 150 to 250 calories per hour. This rule of thumb changes for longer distance racing, a discussion saved for another book.

Run

Since you have not been running much longer than 10 minutes, you will begin your running program with a 10-minute run. To prevent injury, it is important for you to have a pair of proper running shoes before beginning the program. Go to a store that specializes in running shoes and work with a knowledgeable store employee to get a shoe model that is right for you. Too often, people think their old standby shoes, worn for activities and general errands the past 5 years, are good enough. They are not.

The first two Tuesday runs are 10 minutes long. Yes, only 10 minutes and only Zone 1. The first two Saturday runs are 15 minutes long and are at Zone 1 intensity. In Weeks 3 through 11, Tuesday is either a day off or a run at Zones 1 to 2 intensity. Saturday running workouts build in duration to 30 minutes and gently build to Zone 3 intensity. Saturday runs also include form work. As with swimming and cycling, you want to use good form to improve running economy. Two drills are included in this plan to improve form:

Cadence: Run a flat to gently rolling course at intensity Zones 1 to 2. No need to push Zone 2. Within the run, check leg speed a few times by counting your left (or right) foot strikes for 15 seconds. The total should be 21 or more. Running cadence is similar to cycling cadence in that it refers to the number of times per minute your right (or left) foot completes one cycle of motion.

Accels: Within a run that is mostly Zones 1 to 2 intensity, insert several 20- to 30-second accelerations when the mood strikes you. Finish each acceleration faster than you began. Quick cadence and proud posture are important. Feel light and fast. Jog easy for 2 or more minutes between accelerations.

Bricks

The plan reduces training volume each third week so you can rest, recover, and get stronger. The Saturday workout during each rest week is a brick—a bike ride immediately followed by a run. Brick workouts train your legs to switch from a cycling motion to a running motion. The bricks are also a good opportunity to work on your transition. Since the time it takes you to change from cycling gear to running gear is included in your overall race time, it is in your best interest to minimize transition time.

Practice organizing your gear to facilitate smooth transitions during each brick workout. One good technique for improving your transitions is to have someone videotape your transitions, then review the action later to look for ways to improve.

Race Week

A sure sign of a beginner "tri-nerd" is the guy or gal who tries out the event venue the day before the race. Yes, these people do a practice race on their own—just to be sure they can successfully complete each leg of the event. How do you think someone might feel on race day after having completed the race distance the day before? Tired! Resist the temptation to do a practice event. Save your energy for race day. You will have a much better opportunity for success on race day if you are rested.

If you want to review the course, get a map and take a drive, beginning at the swim. Have a look at the entrance and exit to the swim. From the exit of the swim to the transition area, is the trek long or short? Is the path between the swim and transition area smooth or rocky? Are your feet tender or can you run across a gravel road without blinking an eye? One athlete I coach, Cathy, can run across nearly any surface with no problems. Trekking across uneven grass while barefooted makes me look like I'm running across hot coals. I usually stash running shoes or slip-on shoes at the exit of the swim.

When you drive the bike course, take note of turns, tricky corners, potholes, and hills. In most races, the course is clearly marked and each corner usually has a volunteer standing by to give you directions. However, it is every racer's responsibility to know the course. This means if you get off course, for any reason, you are the responsible party.

Many times you will not know entrance and exit details for the bike-to-run transition until race day. When you arrive on race morning, make a mental note of where your bike is racked (look for landmarks such as a tree or a sign). Where do you enter the transition area from the swim, exit on the bike, enter on the bike, and exit on the run? One of my favorite recommendations for an in-transition marker is the ugliest towel you can find. This ugly towel serves to locate your bike as well as to wipe dirt and rocks off the bottoms of your feet.

Keep your intensity on race day in Zones 1 to 3, the same intensity you have practiced during training. Resist the temptation to try new equipment or new, miracle performance enhancers on race day. Stick with what has been working for you and save the new stuff as an experiment for your next training day.

Table 5.1 Fit Beginner Plan for a Sprint Distance Triathlon

Week	Monday	Tuesday	Wednesday	Thursday
1	Strength AA 30–45 min. OR Day off	Run 10 min. Zone 1	Swim 10 x 50 (45 sec. RI) Zone 1	Bike 30 min. with spin-ups Zones 1–2
2	Strength AA 30–45 min. OR Day off	Run 10 min. Zone 1	Swim 10 x 50 (30 sec. RI) Zone 1	Bike 30 min. with ILT work Zones 1–2
3	Strength AA 30 min. OR Day off	Day off	Swim 10 x 50 (10 sec. RI) Zone 1	Bike 30 min. at 90 rpm Zones 1–2
4	Strength SM 30–45 min. OR Day off	Run 15 min. Zones 1–2	Swim 10 x 50 (15 sec. RI) Zones 1–2	Bike 30 min. with spin-ups Zones 1–2
5	Strength SM 30–45 min. OR Day off	Run 15 min. Zones 1–2	Swim 10 x 50 (10 sec. RI) Zones 1–2	Bike 30 min. with ILT work Zones 1–2
6	Strength SM 30 min. OR Day off	Day off	Swim 200 steady, rest 1 min. 10 x 25 (15 sec. RI), odds EZ, evens fast Zones 1–2	Bike 30 min. at 90 rpm Zones 1–2
7	Strength SM 30–45 min. OR Day off	Run 20 min. Zones 1–2	Swim 10–12 x 50 (30 sec. RI), odds EZ, evens fast Zones 1–3	Bike 30 min. with spin-ups Zones 1–2
8	Strength SM 30–45 min. OR Day off	Run 20 min. Zones 1–2	Swim 10–12 x 50 (30 sec. RI), odds EZ, evens fast Zones 1–3	Bike 30 min. with ILT work Zones 1–2
9	Strength SM 30 min. OR Day off	Day off	Swim 300 steady, rest 1 min then 6–8 x 25 (15 sec. RI), odds EZ, evens fast Zones 1–3	Bike 30 min. at 90 rpm Zones 1–2
10	Strength SM 30–45 min. OR Day off	Run 20 min. Zones 1–2	Swim 10–12 x 50 (2 easy, 2 fast), repeat pattern (30 sec. RI), Zones 1–2	Bike 30 min. with spin-ups Zones 1–2
11	Strength SM 30–45 min. OR Day off	Run 20 min. Zones 1–2	Swim 10–12 x 50 (2 easy, 2 fast), repeat pattern (30 sec. RI) Zones 1–2	Bike 30 min. with ILT work Zones 1–2
12	Day off	Run 15 min. Zones 1–2 Include a few 20-sec. accels	Swim 10 x 50 (25 yd. easy, 25 yd. at race pace), repeat pattern (30 sec. RI) Zones 1–2	Bike 30 min. at 90 rpm Zones 1–2

Friday	Saturday	Sunday	Weekly Totals
Swim 10 x 50 (30 sec. RI) Zone 1	**Run** 15 min. Zone 1	**Bike** 30 min. Zone 1 Flat course	2 hr.– 2 hr., 45 min.
Swim 10 x 50 (20 sec. RI) Zone 1	**Run** 15 min. Zone 1	**Bike** 45 min. Zone 1 Flat course	2 hr., 30 min.– 3 hr.
Day off	**BRICK** **Bike** 20–30 min. **Run** 10–15 min. Zone 1	Day off	2 hr.– 2 hr., 15 min.
Swim 8 x 75 (20 sec. RI) Zones 1–2	**Run** 20 min. Zones 1–2 Cadence	**Bike** 1 hr. Zones 1–2 Rolling course	3 hr.– 3 hr., 30 min.
Swim 5–7 x 100 (20 sec. RI) Zones 1–2	**Run** 20 min. Zones 1–2 Cadence	**Bike** 1 hr., 15 min. Zones 1–2 Rolling course	3 hr., 15 min.– 3 hr., 45 min.
Day off	**BRICK** **Bike** 30–45 min. **Run** 15–20 min. Zones 1–2	Day off	2 hr.– 2 hr., 15 min.
Swim 1 x 200 (20 sec. RI), 3–5 x 100 (10 sec. RI) Zones 1–2	**Run** 30 min. Zones 1–3 Accels	**Bike** 1 hr., 30 min. Zones 1–3 Terrain similar to race	3 hr., 45 min.– 4 hr., 15 min.
Swim 2 x 200 (20 sec. RI), 2–4 x 100 (10 sec. RI) Zones 1–2	**Run** 30 min. Zones 1–3 Accels	**Bike** 1 hr., 45 min. Zones 1–3 Terrain similar to race	4 hr.– 4 hr., 30 min.
Day off	**BRICK** **Bike** 60–75 min. **Run** 20–30 min. Zones 1–3	Day off	2 hr.– 2 hr., 15 min.
Swim 500 steady at race pace (1 min. RI) Zones 1–3 Optional: Add 4–6 x 50 (20 sec. RI)	**Run** 30–40 min. Zones 1–3 Accels	**Bike** 2 hr. Zones 1–3 Terrain similar to race	4 hr., 30 min.– 5 hr.
Swim 500 steady at race pace (1 min. RI) Zones 1–3 Optional: Add 4–6 x 50 (20 sec. RI)	**Run** 30–40 min. Zones 1–3 Accels	**Bike** 1 hr., 30 min., Zones 1–3 Terrain similar to race	3 hr., 45 min.– 4 hr., 15 min.
Day off	**Bike** 20–30 min. Zones 1–2 **OR** Day off	Race	1 hr.– 1 hr., 30 min. + race time

Chapter 6

Unfit Beginner
Plan for an Olympic Distance Triathlon

To be a warrior is not a simple matter of wishing to be one.
It is rather an endless struggle that will go on to the very last moment of our lives.
Nobody is born a warrior, in exactly the same way that nobody is born an average
man. We make ourselves into one or the other.
—Carlos Castaneda, Twentieth-Century Mystic and Toltec Warrior,
from Tales of Power

While it's nice to make your triathlon debut at a sprint distance event, it's not always convenient or possible. For example, a nearby town or city might host a great Olympic distance race and the date of the event fits nicely into your busy calendar. Although the event sounds like a lot of fun you wonder, "Do I have the time to train for that event? Can I really complete an Olympic distance race or am I fooling myself?"

It doesn't take as much time to train for an Olympic distance event as you might think. With a solid training plan, you can successfully complete the event. It may help to know the weekly total training hours for the plan range from 1 hour, 45 minutes to around 7 hours, 30 minutes. Yes, that is all the training time you need. Are you more interested now?

Interested, yes, but you might think, "I'm not the fastest horse in the barn, so that training plan cannot possibly be for me." On the contrary. Do you think you can swim 1,500 meters, averaging 2 minutes to 2 minutes, 45 seconds per 100 meters? Can you ride a bike for 24.8 miles, averaging between 15 and 18 miles per hour? How about running (or run/walk) 6.2 miles, averaging between 9 and 15 minutes per mile? If these numbers sound realistic, it is possible for you to complete an Olympic distance event in the 3- to 4-hour range.

To get a better estimate of your total predicted finish time, Table 6.1 provides a pace chart. For each sport, a pace range is listed. Each pace has a corresponding estimated completion time for that particular event. By adding the various completion times in each column, it is possible to see how an athlete who is a strong cyclist and a weak runner might have a similar completion time to an athlete who is a weak cyclist and a strong runner. Both athletes can use the same plan to guide their training.

Before getting into the specifics of the plan, I'll outline the goal and an athlete profile for the person for whom this plan is designed.

Goal

Comfortably complete an Olympic distance triathlon consisting of approximately 1,500 meters of swimming, 40 kilometers (24.8 miles) of cycling, and 10 kilometers (6.2 miles) of running and/or walking. The target completion time is around 3 or 4 hours.

Profile

You are a beginning triathlete, more concerned with completing the event comfortably rather than with setting a sea- and land-speed record. Your schedule allows you to train 30 to 45 minutes on most weekdays, and you must have 1 day totally free from training to pursue other activities. On weekends, your training time is more flexible. However, the maximum amount of time you want to put into a single training day is about 3 hours.

Before beginning Week 1 on the training chart, you are capable of swimming 50 meters without stopping and can comfortably cycle 30 to 60 minutes. Throughout the plan, two options are provided for the running segment of the event. The first option is a run/walk option. If

Table 6.1 Pace Chart for Olympic Distance Racing

Swim 1,500 meters		Bike 24.8 miles		Run 6.2 miles	
Pace per 100 meters (hr.:min.:sec.)	Split time (hr.:min.)	Pace (mph)	Split time (hr.:min.)	Pace per mile (min.)	Split time (hr.:min.)
0:02:00	0:30	20	1:14	9	0:56
0:02:15	0:34	19	1:18	10	1:02
0:02:30	0:38	18	1:23	11	1:08
0:02:45	0:41	17	1:28	12	1:15
0:03:00	0:45	16	1:33	13	1:21
0:03:15	0:49	15	1:40	14	1:27
0:03:30	0:53	14	1:46	15	1:33

Transitions can be estimated at 5 minutes each.

using the run/walk option, you are currently capable of running for a minute and walking for a minute, repeating the sequence seven or eight times. The second option given throughout the plan is for runners. Before beginning the plan, runners can easily run or jog for 15 to 20 minutes, nonstop.

If you happen to have more endurance than described in the last paragraph, you can consider beginning the plan in a later week. If you begin the training deeper into the plan, the first week of training you aim for should look easy to accomplish.

If your fitness is lower than the criteria for beginning Week 1 training, you need to improve your fitness before beginning the plan. How to gain that base fitness is not covered in this book.

With the goal and profile in mind, look at the first 4 weeks of the plan. (See Table 6.2 at the end of this chapter.) Notice that weekly training ranges from 1 hour, 45 minutes to 3 hours, 45 minutes. The maximum weekly training hours for the plan is 7 hours, 30 minutes and occurs in Week 10. The plan shows Friday as a day off. If it is more convenient for you to take off a different day, simply move the workouts accordingly. In general, try to put swim workouts at least 48 hours apart from one another and apply the same rule of thumb to cycling or running.

For all the workouts, use a rating of perceived exertion (RPE) to judge intensity and speed. This RPE is referred to by "zone." When working with endurance athletes, I often use heart rate monitors, power or specific speed intervals in addition to RPE; but those tools are not used in this training plan. (See Chapter 3 for a discussion of RPE and training zones.)

The Plan

The plan in Table 6.2 has a general pattern of cycling on Monday and Saturday, swimming on Tuesday and Thursday, running on Wednesday and Sunday, with Friday as a day off. If it is more convenient for you to have a different schedule, feel free to move the workouts around. Try to keep similar workouts 48 hours apart. In other words, it is preferable to swim on Tuesday and Thursday instead of Tuesday and Wednesday.

If you are currently strength training, you can keep your current routine. Pay attention to whether or not strength training is taking too much energy away from your swimming, cycling, and running. If this is the case, consider reducing the exercises, sets, or repetitions to allow higher-quality workouts during the aerobic sessions. Another option for strength training is to use the routine listed in Chapter 12.

Swim

The plan shows a minimum amount of swimming to help you complete the event successfully. If you have a swimming background, you may want to add more warm-up and/or cool-down yards to what is shown in Table 6.2. The general strategy of the plan is to begin by swimming 50-yard (or 50-meter) repeats, with generous rest, totaling 500 yards. (Most standard pools are either 25 yards or 25 meters long. Ask the lifeguard how long your pool is if you are not sure.) As the plan progresses, the length of your swims increases and rest decreases. You are building endurance.

For example, on Tuesday of Week 1, swim ten repeats of 50 yards, taking a 20-second rest interval (20 sec. RI) between each swim. The swim should feel easy, Zone 1 intensity. By Tuesday of Week 3, you swim fourteen repeats of 50 yards, resting only 15 seconds between each swim.

The Thursday swims are slightly faster, including swimming in Zones 1 and 2. If you are feeling tired, keep the intensity low. If you feel spunky, include some Zone 2 swimming.

Week 4 is a reduced-volume week for recovery. The daily workout pattern changes some, beginning with swimming 5 x 100 meters on Tuesday, resting 20 seconds between each 100. On Saturday, you can complete the swim as a solo workout, then bike and run later in the day. Or you can do a race simulation day, doing all three workouts in close succession. Either way, swim 500 meters nonstop for the swim workout. If you need to stop and catch your breath a couple of times during the 500, try to minimize rest time.

In Weeks 5 through 8, the Tuesday swim workout is 50s and the Thursday workout has longer sets, 100s and 200s. The Tuesday swims should be just a bit faster, to include some Zone 3 swimming, while Thursday is Zones 1 to 2 only.

The first workout in Week 5 is to swim 16 x 50 meters, resting about 20 seconds between each 50 meters. The Thursday workout for that week is to swim 6 x 100 meters, resting about 20 seconds between each 100. The workouts follow a similar pattern for Week 6.

In Week 7, the Tuesday main-set swim is broken into two segments. You will swim 10 x 50 meters, resting 15 seconds between each 50. After the tenth swim, take 2 minutes to recover and do a second set of 10 x 50 meters. The Thursday swim in Week 7 contains 200s in the main set. Swim five repeats of 200 meters, resting 20 to 30 seconds between each 200.

Week 8 is a reduced-volume week for recovery. The daily workout pattern changes some, beginning with swimming 6 x 100 meters on Tuesday, resting 20 seconds between each 100. On Saturday, similar to Week 4, you can complete the swim as a solo workout, then bike and run later in the day or do a race simulation day. Either way, swim 1,000 meters nonstop for the Saturday swim workout. If you need to stop and catch your breath a couple of times during the swim, try to minimize rest time.

In Weeks 9 through 12, the Tuesday swim remains slightly faster, to include some Zone 3 swimming, while Thursday remains in Zones 1 to 2. The first workout in Week 9 is to swim three sets of 6 to 8 x 50 meters, resting about 15 seconds between each 50-meter swim. After completing six to eight repetitions, take a full minute to recover before beginning your second trip, though. After the second set, take a full minute to rest before completing the third set. The Thursday workout for that week is to swim 4 x 300 meters, resting 20 to 30 seconds between each 300, *or* swim 1,200 nonstop. If your race is in open water, consider swimming in a safe open-water situation for about the time it would take you to complete 1,200 meters of swimming. (A safe open-water situation is one where a lifeguard or boat is watching you.)

The workouts follow a similar pattern for Week 10, with the Tuesday main-set swims being shorter than Thursday swims. On Tuesday, there are still three sets, but swim 8 to 10 x 50 meters for each set. The Thursday workout for Week 10 is to swim 3 x 400 meters, resting about 20 seconds between each 400, or swim 1,200 nonstop.

In Week 11, the Tuesday main-set swim is 8 x 100 meters, resting 30 seconds between each 100. The final long swim prior to race day is Thursday of Week 11. Swim 3 x 500 meters, with 20 to 30 seconds between each 500, *or* swim a continuous 1,500 meters.

Notice that Week 11 is a reduced-volume week to begin tapering your workouts for race day. The Saturday workout is similar to the workout you did during Weeks 4 and 8. A good strategy is to make this workout a race simulation day by putting all three workouts in close succession. Swim 500 to 800 meters nonstop, transition to the 1-hour bike ride, and finally transition to a 30-minute run or a pattern of running 9 minutes, walking 1 minute. The entire workout is at an intensity within Zones 1 to 3.

A good strategy for this race simulation and for race day is to make the intensity in the first half of the time, in each sport, in Zones 1 to 2. Make the second half of the time in each sport in Zones 1 to 3. Include more Zone 3 time if you are feeling strong and energetic. This strategy, called "negative-split," keeps you from going out too fast and "blowing up."

Bike

The bike workout pattern for Weeks 1 through 3 includes an easy ride on Monday, lasting 30 to 45 minutes, and a longer ride of about 60 minutes on Saturday. The Saturday ride can include more speed. The rides should be on flat to gently rolling courses. It is best to ride steady and at a moderate to easy pace.

For your long rides, carry water and practice drinking while riding. Because the long rides build to over an hour, fueling and hydrating are critical. This is covered later in the chapter.

As mentioned in the "Swim" section, the Saturday workout in Week 4 can be used as a race simulation day. Complete the swim as already described, then go right to a bike ride of about an hour. Immediately after the bike ride, run a steady 30 minutes or complete the run/walk pattern. (Run and run/walk patterns are described in the "Run" section.) A bike ride immediately followed by a run is typically called a "brick." Practicing the transitions from swimming to cycling and from cycling to running helps you work out the bugs prior to race day. Keep in mind that the transition times are included in your overall race time.

The bike workout pattern for Weeks 5 through 8 includes a form ride on Monday, lasting 45 to 60 minutes, and a longer ride on Saturday. For the form ride, the RPE is Zones 1 to 2. For the spin-ups, keep the gearing such that it is easy to spin the cranks at high revolutions per minute (rpm). Shoot for 30 rpm or more in 20 seconds. Try to spin high rpm while keeping your torso quiet—no swinging shoulders or bouncing butt on the bike seat. The goal is to improve pedaling economy with this workout, and you want relaxed speed.

The Saturday ride in Weeks 5 through 8 can include more intensity. The ride can be on a flat, gently rolling, or a moderately hilly course. This endurance-building ride is in Zones 1 to 3. It is *not* your goal to maximize Zone 3 time.

For long workouts (those longer than an hour), carry a sports drink or water, supplemented with an energy bar. Many athletes do carry water for the shorter workouts as well. Stay hydrated by drinking approximately one bike bottle per hour of training or racing. You need to fuel yourself with approximately 150 to 300 calories per hour for Olympic distance racing. Some of the larger athletes may need slightly more fuel. Select an energy drink or bar that is high in carbohydrates. The fuel can contain some protein and fat, but those ingredients should be minimized.

The purpose of hydrating and fueling during training and the event is to keep your body running at optimal levels. Even relatively low levels of dehydration affect performance and recovery. As for fueling, the body can store enough glycogen to get you through about 90 minutes of exercise. Some of your training periods, and certainly the race, will last more than 90 minutes, so you need to supplement your body's stored fuel.

A good idea is to practice your fueling and hydrating techniques on a regular schedule, within a workout. For example, plan to fuel and hydrate at 15- to 20-minute intervals during a workout. Beginning at the 20- or 30-minute mark, early and steady fueling and hydrating prevent the dreaded "bonk." "Bonk" is the term that describes when your body is running low on glycogen stores. When you bonk, you feel like you are working quite hard but getting nowhere. A general fatigue seems to envelop your body. It is best for body and spirit to avoid bonking.

The bike workout pattern for Weeks 9 through 11 continues with a form ride on Monday in Zones 1 to 2, lasting 45 to 60 minutes. Weeks 9 and 10 include a longer ride on Saturday in Zones 1 to 3. The long rides in Weeks 9 and 10 are best done on a course that is similar in profile to what you will face on race day.

Run

Each run workout description begins with the planned approximate total time for the entire workout. For example, the total run time for Tuesday of Week 2 is shown as 25 minutes. The detail of the workout shows the run/walk workout as run 1 minute and walk 1 minute, repeated twelve to fourteen times to total some 24 to 28 minutes. Also notice the word "total" is eliminated after Week 3.

There are generally two options shown for the run workouts. The first option is for athletes wanting to ease back gently into running or for athletes intending to use a run/walk pattern on race day. Using a combination of walking and running in the event is a great strategy. In the first run workout shown on Wednesday of Week 1, run 1 minute and walk 1 minute; repeat the sequence seven or eight times. In the Sunday workout, run 1 minute and walk 1 minute; repeat the sequence nine or ten times.

Wednesday runs during Weeks 1 through 4 are all in Zone 1 or very easy intensity. Sunday runs can include more speed, Zones 1 to 2, but they are not intended to be killer-fast. None of the workouts shown in the plan should leave you feeling exhausted.

The second option shown on run days is a steady run time. For example, on Wednesday of Week 1, the second option is to run 15 minutes at a steady, easy pace.

Whether you decide to run or do a combination of running and walking, it is important to begin the program with good running shoes. The shoes do not have to be the most expensive ones in the store, but be sure they fit and are designed for running. An expert in a good running gear store can help you find the right shoe.

Moving to the workout on Wednesday of Week 5, run 4 minutes and walk 1 minute; repeat the sequence six times. Intensity opens up to Zones 1 to 2. The Sunday workout is run 6 minutes and walk 1 minute; repeat the sequence four times. Sunday endurance runs or run/walk workouts are at intensity Zones 1 to 3, but again they are not meant to be killer-fast. Do not attempt to maximize Zone 3 on these runs.

As in Weeks 1 to 4, the second option shown on the run days is steady run time. For example, on Wednesday of Week 5, the second option is to run 15 minutes at a steady, easy pace in Zones 1 to 2.

The running plan changes slightly in Weeks 9 through 12 in that runners can include a few 20-second accelerations (accels) during the Wednesday workouts. Accelerations are not all-out running, but rather a gentle build of speed and increasing cadence. If you decide to include them, do 4 x to 5 x 20-second accelerations, resting 1 minute, 40 seconds between each acceleration.

Race Week

For race week, Week 12, do not be tempted to exceed the volume shown in the plan. Stick to the plan and race day will be much more enjoyable, because you will be rested. On Monday of Week 12, complete a brick consisting of a 45-minute bike ride, immediately followed by a 15-minute run or a run/walk pattern of running 7 minutes and walking 1 minute. The entire workout is in Zones 1 to 2.

The Wednesday brick is a very short bike ride of 20 minutes, followed by a 10-minute (yes, that's all) run or run/walk. If you run/walk, complete 4 minutes of running, followed by 30 seconds of walking, and repeat that sequence twice.

The Tuesday workout in Week 12 is to swim 8 x 100 meters, resting 30 seconds between each 100 at intensity Zones 1 to 2. The Thursday swim is 8 x 50 meters, resting 20 seconds between each 50, swum at your projected race intensity.

Friday of Week 12 is a rest day and Saturday is a short bike ride of only 30 minutes. On Saturday, ride in mostly Zone 1 and try out all the gears to make sure they are working properly. After this ride, you are officially ready. It is time to relax and put your feet up.

If your race is on Saturday instead of Sunday, then do your bike check during the Wednesday brick and keep the rest of the schedule as is. You can take Sunday as a day off, or an easy spin or easy swim is fine.

On race morning, be sure to give yourself plenty of time to drive to the event, allowing for traffic jams. Depending on the size of the race, 300 to 2,000 people are all trying to get to the same parking lot, and it is usually reached by the same road. Most athletes also need to plan for at least one trip to the porta-potty and the associated wait in line.

When you finally get to the starting queue, take a deep breath and try to relax. This is supposed to be fun. Race at the same intensity as your training events and you will have a great race.

Table 6.2 Unfit Beginner Plan for an Olympic Distance Triathlon

Week	Monday	Tuesday	Wednesday	Thursday
1	Bike 30 min. Zone 1	Swim 10 x 50 (20 sec. RI) Zone 1	Run/Walk 15 min.: 7–8 x (run 1 min., walk 1 min.), Zone 1 OR Run 15 min. steady Zone 1	Swim 10 x 50 (20 sec. RI) Zones 1–2
2	Bike 45 min. Zone 1	Swim 12 x 50 (20 sec. RI) Zone 1	Run/Walk 25 min.: 12–14 x (run 1 min., walk 1 min.), Zone 1 OR Run 25 min. steady Zone 1	Swim 12 x 50 (20 sec. RI) Zones 1–2
3	Bike 45 min. Zone 1	Swim 14 x 50 (15 sec. RI) Zone 1	Run/Walk 30 min.: 10 x (run 2 min., walk 1 min.), Zone 1 OR Run 15 min. steady Zone 1	Swim 14 x 50 (15 sec. RI) Zones 1–2
4	Day off	Swim 5 x 100 (20 sec. RI) Zone 1	Run/Walk 15 min.: 3 x (run 4 min., walk 1 min.), Zone 1 OR Run 15 min. steady Zone 1	Bike 45 min. Zone 1
5	Bike 45–60 min. with 4–6 x 20 sec. spin-ups (1 min., 40 sec. RI) Zones 1–2	Swim 16 x 50 (15 sec. RI) Zones 1–3	Run/Walk 30 min.: 6 x (run 4 min., walk 1 min.), Zones 1–2 OR Run 15 min. steady Zones 1–2	Swim 6 x 100 (20 sec. RI) Zones 1–2
6	Bike 45–60 min. with 6–8 x 20 sec. spin-ups (1 min., 40 sec. RI) Zones 1–2	Swim 18 x 50 (15 sec. RI) Zones 1–3	Run/Walk 32 min.: 4 x (run 7 min., walk 1 min.), Zones 1–2 OR Run 30 min. steady Zones 1–2	Swim 6–8 x 100 (20 sec. RI) Zones 1–2
7	Bike 45–60 min. with 8–10 x 20 sec. spin-ups (1 min., 40 sec. RI) Zones 1–2	Swim 10 x 50 (15 sec. RI), 2 min. bonus rest 10 x 50 (15 sec. RI) Zones 1–3	Run/Walk 30 min.: 3 x (run 9 min., walk 1 min.), Zones 1–2 OR Run 30 min. steady Zones 1–2	Swim 5 x 200 (20–30 sec. RI) Zones 1–2
8	Day off	Swim 6–8 x 100 (20 sec. RI) Zones 1–3	Run/Walk 15 min.: 3 x (run 4 min., walk 1 min.), Zones 1–2 OR Run 15 min. steady Zones 1–2	Bike 45 min. Zone 1
9	Bike 45–60 min. with 4–6 x 30 sec. spin-ups (1 min., 30 sec. RI) Zones 1–2	Swim 6–8 x 50 (15 sec. RI) x 3 with 1 min. bonus rest after each set	Run/Walk 30 min.: 3 x (run 9 min., walk 1 min.), Zones 1–2 OR Run 30 min. steady with 4 x 20 sec. accels (1 min., 40 sec. RI)	Swim 4 x 300 (20–30 sec. RI) OR Swim 1,200 steady
10	Bike 45–60 min. with 6–8 x 30 sec. spin-ups (1 min., 30 sec. RI) Zones 1–2	Swim 8–10 x 50 (15 sec. RI) x 3 with 1 min. bonus rest after each set	Run/Walk 30 min.: 3 x (run 9 min., walk 1 min.), Zones 1–2 OR Run 30 min. steady with 4–5 x 20 sec. accels (1 min., 40 sec. RI)	Swim 3 x 400 (20–30 sec. RI) OR Swim 1,200 steady
11	Bike 45 min. with 4–6 x 30 sec. spin-ups (1 min., 30 sec. RI) Zones 1–2	Swim 8 x 100 (30 sec. RI)	Run/Walk 30 min.: 3 x (run 9 min., walk 1 min.), Zones 1–2 OR Run 30 min. steady with 4–5 x 20 sec. accels (1 min., 40 sec. RI)	Swim 3 x 500 (20–30 sec. RI) OR Swim 1,500 steady
12	BRICK Bike 30 min., Run 15 min. Total time 45 min. Zones 1–2	Swim 8 x 100 (30 sec. RI) Zones 1–2	BRICK Bike 20 min., Run 10 min. Total time 30 min. Zones 1–2	Swim 8 x 50 (20 sec. RI) Zones 1–2

Friday	Saturday	Sunday	Weekly Totals
Day off	Bike 1 hr. Zones 1–2	Run/Walk 20 min.: 9–10 x (run 1 min., walk 1 min.), Zones 1–2 OR Run 20 min. steady Zones 1–2	2 hr., 45 min.
Day off	Bike 1 hr. Zones 1–2	Run/Walk 30 min.: 15 x (run 1 min., walk 1 min.), Zones 1–2 OR Run 30 min. steady Zones 1–2	3 hr., 45 min.
Day off	Bike 1 hr. Zones 1–2	Run/Walk 30 min.: 7–8 x (run 3 min., walk 1 min.), Zones 1–2 OR Run 30 min. steady Zones 1–2	3 hr., 35 min.
Day off	Swim 500 steady, Zones 1–2 Bike 1 hr., Zones 1–2 Run 30 min. steady OR (Run 2 min., walk 1 min.) x 10 Zones 1–2	Day off	1 hr., 45 min.
Day off	Bike 1–1.5 hr. Zones 1–3	Run/Walk 30–45 min.: 4–6 x (run 6 min., walk 1 min.), Zones 1–3 OR Run 30–45 min. steady Zones 1–3	3 hr., 45 min.–4 hr., 45 min.
Day off	Bike 1.5–2 hr. Zones 1–3	Run/Walk 30–45 min.: 3–4 x (run 8 min., walk 1 min.), Zones 1–3 OR Run 30–45 min. steady Zones 1–3	4 hr., 15 min.–5 hr., 15 min.
Day off	Bike 2–2.5 hr. Zones 1–3	Run/Walk 40–50 min.: 4–5 x (run 9 min., walk 1 min.), Zones 1–3 OR Run 45 min. steady Zones 1–3	5 hr.–5 hr., 45 min.
Day off	Swim 1,000 steady, Zones 1–2 Bike 1.5 hr., Zones 1–2 Run 30 min. steady OR (Run 2 min., walk 1 min.) x 10 Zones 1–2	Day off	3 hr., 30 min.
Day off	Bike 2.5–3 hr. Zones 1–3	Run/Walk 50–60 min.: 5–6 x (run 9 min., walk 1 min.), Zones 1–3 OR Run 60 min. steady Zones 1–3	6–7 hr.
Day off	Bike 3–3.5 hr. Zones 1–3	Run/Walk 1 hr.: 6 x (run 9 min., walk 1 min.), Zones 1–3 OR Run 60 min. steady Zones 1–3	6 hr., 45 min.–7 hr., 30 min.
Day off	Swim 500–800 steady Bike 1 hr., Zones 1–3 Run 30 min. steady, Zones 1–3 OR (Run 2 min., walk 1 min.) x 10	Day off	4 hr., 30 min.
Day off	Bike 30 min. Mostly easy, run through your gears	Race	2 hr., 45 min. + race time

Chapter 7

Fit Beginner

Plan for an Olympic Distance Triathlon

You are never given a wish without also being given the power to make it true.
You may have to work for it, however.
—Richard Bach, from *Illusions: The Adventures of a Reluctant Messiah*

The Fit Beginner Plan for Olympic distance racing can be used as a progression from the Unfit Beginner Plan or as a starting point for a fit beginner. The first week of the plan shown in Table 7.1 has a long run of 45 minutes and a long bike ride ranging from 2 hours to 2 hours, 30 minutes. (See table at the end of this chapter.) This level offers a good rebuilding point for someone who has completed the plan in Chapter 6 and who is ready for the next level of fitness. If you already consider yourself fit, the first week of the plan in Table 7.1 should look easy. If you think Week 1 looks too challenging, consider beginning with the plan in Chapter 6. Depending on your current fitness level, you may be capable of beginning with Week 5 in the Chapter 6 plan until you build enough fitness to jump to the Chapter 7 plan.

Goal

Comfortably complete an Olympic distance triathlon consisting of approximately 1,500 meters (0.9 mile) of swimming , 40 kilometers (24.8 miles) of cycling, and 10 kilometers (6.2 miles) of running or walking.

Profile

You are a beginning triathlete, but not a beginning athlete. Before beginning Week 1 of the plan, you are capable of riding a bike 30 to 60 minutes 2 days a week and completing a long ride of about 2 hours on a third day. You can swim 100 yards (or meters) nonstop, and swimming for 30 minutes a couple of times per week is easy for you. You can run 2 days per week—one 30-minute run and a longer run of 45 minutes.

If you happen to have more endurance than described in the last paragraph, you can consider beginning the plan in a later week. If you begin the training at a later week in the plan, the first week of training you aim for should look easy to accomplish.

With the goal and profile in mind, look at the plan shown in Table 7.1. Notice that weekly training hours range from 5 hours, 15 minutes to a maximum between 8 hours, 15 minutes and 10 hours. To accommodate individual differences, some flexibility is built into the plan.

The Plan

The plan in Table 7.1 has a general pattern of cycling and strength training on Monday and Wednesday. Strength training is optional in this plan. If you decide not to strength train, you can replace the strength-training time with more time on the bike on those days. Long rides are on Sundays. Swimming is shown on Tuesday, Thursday, and some Saturdays. Running workouts are typically on Tuesday, some Thursdays, and Saturday. Friday is a day off. If you prefer a different schedule, you can move the workouts around. Try to keep similar workouts 48 hours apart. In other words, it is preferable to swim on Tuesday and Thursday instead of Tuesday and Wednesday.

If you are currently strength training, you can keep your current routine. Pay attention to whether or not strength training is taking too much energy away from your swimming, cycling, and running. If it is, consider reducing the exercises, sets, or repetitions to allow higher-quality workouts during the aerobic sessions. Another option for strength training is to use the suggested routine in Table 7.1. (Details of strength training are discussed in Chapter 12.)

For all the workouts in the plan, you can use RPE or heart rate to judge intensity and speed. Your intensity gauge is referred to by "zone." (See Chapter 3 for information on determining RPE and related zones.) With or without a heart rate monitor, it is valuable for all athletes to develop RPE.

Swim

The swimming workouts are addressed separately from those for biking and running. Due to the space it would take to list thirty-six swimming workouts, a repeating workout set is listed in this chapter. The workouts are designated as 1, 2, and 3 in Table 7.1. If you prefer more variety for your workouts, ideas for main sets can be found in Chapters 6, 10, and 11. Another good resource for more detailed workouts is the waterproof book *Workouts in a Binder: Swim Workouts for Triathletes* by Gale Bernhardt and Nick Hansen (VeloPress, 2003).

The workouts in this chapter nicely suit a swimmer who can swim 100 yards (or meters) in 1 minute, 30 seconds to 2 minutes. The instructions do not designate yards or meters: You can use them interchangeably for this chapter. Detailed instructions for swimming form and drills are not included in this book.

In the workouts listed in this chapter, a range of yards is shown in the main set; for example, 6–8 x 50 (or six to eight repeats of lengths of 50 yards). If you are just getting back into swimming, begin with fewer repetitions. As you progress through the plan, there may be days when you need more recovery. On those days, it is a good idea to aim for the lower number of repetitions. Making adjustments to the workouts in any plan, to balance recovery and build fitness, is key for a self-coached athlete.

Definitions for Swim Workouts

Swim: Swim any stroke; use primarily freestyle.
Kick: With or without a kickboard, kick only.

Drill: Your choice of drills. Examples include single-arm swimming, closed-fist swimming, fingertip drag during recovery, catch-up drill, etc.

RI: Rest interval between swims.

Warm-up: Preparing the body to swim.

Main set: The focus of the workout.

Cooldown: Swimming easy to begin the recovery process.

Workout 1

    Warm-up: 200 swim, 200 kick, 200 drill

    Main set: 6–8 x 50 (10-second RI between swims). Swim at Zones 1 to 2 RPE.

    Cooldown: 200 your choice

Workout 2

    Warm-up: 2 x (100 swim, 100 kick, 100 drill)

    Main set: 3–5 x 100 (15–20-second RI between swims). Swim at Zones 1 to 2 RPE.

    Cooldown: 200 your choice

Workout 3

    Warm-up: 500 your choice, mixed swim, drill, and kick

    Main set: 4–8 x 200, take a 20-second RI between swims. Swim at Zones 1 to 3 RPE.

              4–6 x 50, take a 30-second RI between swims. Make each swim faster than the previous one.

    Cooldown: 200 your choice

The workout sets for swimming can be used throughout the entire 12 weeks.

Strength

Similar to swimming, strength training is addressed separately from cycling and running. As mentioned earlier in the chapter, you can use your own strength-training routine, use the routine suggested and detailed in Chapter 12, or eliminate strength training and add more cycling time on the days when strength training is displayed.

Week 1

Because swimming and strength training were addressed in the previous section, the remainder of the chapter looks at weekly details of cycling and running workouts.

Bike

The weekday bike rides are form workouts to improve pedaling technique. Improved technique improves economy. In short, improving economy gives you more speed for a given effort level. There are three workouts designed to improve your pedaling economy:

Spin-ups: After a warm-up, gently increase your cadence over the course of 30 seconds or so. "Cadence" refers to the number of times one of your legs completes one revolution of pedaling. You can count the number of times your right (or left) leg is at the bottom of the pedal stroke over the course of 15 seconds and multiply that value by four to get revolutions per minute (rpm). Inexperienced cyclists tend to have a low cadence, 50 rpm, while experienced cyclists have a higher cadence, 80 rpm or more, on a flat course. When your butt begins bouncing off your bicycle seat, reduce your cadence and recover a minute or two before beginning the next spin-up. Complete four to six spin-ups. Be sure to spin easy at the end of the workout.

Isolated leg training (ILT): Isolated leg training improves pedaling technique as you apply force around as much of the pedal stroke as possible. If you are indoors on a wind trainer, you can place a chair on either side of your bicycle to rest one leg while the other leg is working. If you are on the road, simply relax one leg while the other one does the majority of the work. After a warm-up, pedal with one leg for 30 seconds. At the top of the pedal stroke, drive your knee and toes forward. As your foot begins the downward motion, apply pressure to the pedal as if you were scraping mud off your foot on the curb of a street. As your foot moves to the back of the pedal stroke, lift and unweight your foot and prepare to drive your knee and toes forward again. If you have a "dead spot" in your pedal stroke, it becomes obvious immediately during this drill. Think of your foot and leg as the lever mechanism powering an old-style locomotive. You want that lever constantly delivering power to the wheel. When you finish working one leg, switch to the other leg for 30 seconds. After completing one cycle with each leg, spin with both legs for 30 to 60 seconds. Repeat the cycle, accumulating 3 to 5 minutes of ILT pedaling per leg. Be sure to end the session by spinning easy with both legs.

90 rpm: Pedal the entire session at a cadence of 90 revolutions per minute (rpm) or more. If you are unable to pedal at 90, rest for a while and begin again. You are either pedaling at 90 rpm or higher, or you are resting. If you don't have a cadence sensor as part of your bicycle computer, you can count the number of times your right leg reaches the bottom of the pedal stroke in 15 seconds. The number should be 22 or higher.

In Week 1 of the plan, Monday is a 30-minute ride, pedaling at 90 rpm. This workout is a pedaling technique workout and serves as a warm-up for the strength training session. If you decide not to strength train, ride 60 minutes at 90 rpm. Wednesday is similar to Monday, except the pedaling drill changes to spin-ups. Sunday is the long ride to build overall race endurance and cycling endurance. For Week 1, ride 2 hours to 2 hours, 30 minutes on a rolling course in intensity Zones 1 to 2. Your goal is not to maximize Zone 2 time.

For every ride longer than an hour, carry some type of sports drink or water with food or gel. A good rule of thumb for workouts and races less than 3 hours long is to consume approximately 16 to 24 ounces of fluid and 150 to 250 calories per hour. This rule of thumb changes for longer distance racing, a discussion saved for another book.

Run

The first run shown on Tuesday of Week 1 is 30 minutes long and is an easy run, all at Zone 1 intensity. For the first week, there are only two runs scheduled. The second run is on Saturday and is the long run for the week. Run for 45 minutes at an intensity of Zones 1 to 2.

Week 2

Week 2 is very similar to Week 1. The only changes are the addition of a third swimming workout on Saturday and a 15-minute increase in long run time on Saturday.

Week 3

This is a rest week, with reduced volume. Fitness gains are made by stressing and resting the body. Rest is no less important than work. Monday is a day of rest. Tuesday and Wednesday workouts remain the same as in Weeks 1 and 2. The Thursday brick workout (a bike ride immediately followed by a run) is the beginning of your transition training. On race day, it is important to minimize the time spent in transition. If you use your garage as the transition area, set it up as you would set up your transition area on race day. As you progress through the rest of the training plan, use the brick workout scheduled during rest weeks to improve your transition time. If you do not already have lace locks for your running shoes, pick up a pair. These handy devices eliminate the need to tie your shoes.

For the brick workout itself, bike and run mostly at intensity Zones 1 to 2. After warm-up, include a few 20- to 30-second accelerations in each sport. Four to eight accelerations with easy recovery times of 1 minute, 30 seconds to 1 minute, 40 seconds between each one work well.

The focus of the Sunday brick workout is pace. For both the bike ride and the run, use an out-and-back course and conduct it in a negative-split manner. This means returning the second half of the distance at a slightly faster pace than you began. For Week 3, go out at a speed that elicits Zone 1 heart rate or RPE and come back at Zone 2 intensity. This pace difference is minimal and should not leave you feeling wiped out at the end of the workout.

Week 4

Bike
The weekday bike rides remain form workouts. Monday is the 90 rpm focus and Wednesday is ILT work. (See Week 1 for explanations of the drills.) The long ride on Sunday increases in time, so you are riding 2 hours, 30 minutes to 3 hours. The intensity range opens up some, including time in Zones 1 to 3. Keep Zone 3 time controlled and accumulate 20 to 30 minutes over the course of the entire workout.

Run
The Tuesday run workout time remains at 30 minutes, but intensity increases to Zones 1 and 2. A Thursday run is added. Keep it short at 20 to 30 minutes and keep the intensity in Zones 1 to 2. As with cycling, form is important in running. Count your right (or left) foot strikes and aim for 22 or higher.

The long run time remains at 1 hour and, as in the bike rides, intensity increases to include some Zone 3 time. Don't go wild aiming for an entire run in Zone 3; rather, accumulate about 20 minutes in Zone 3 over the course of the entire run.

Week 5

Bike
The bike pattern for Week 5 is the same as for Week 4. The only change is the amount of time accumulated in Zone 3 during the long ride. Accumulate 30 to 45 minutes of time in Zone 3 during the entire ride.

Run
The weekday run pattern for Week 5 remains the same as for Week 4. However, the long run includes some intervals this week. After a warm-up

mostly in Zones 1 to 2, do four to six intervals that are 5 minutes long. Run the intervals at Zone 3 intensity. Keep in mind it takes some time for your heart rate to respond to the pace. Begin timing the interval as soon as you begin running at Zone 3 pace. After each work interval, jog easy for 2 minutes, getting your heart rate back into Zone 1.

Week 6

The workout pattern for the rest week, Week 6, is the same as for Week 3. Volume is reduced from previous weeks of training, but is increased relative to Week 3. The volume increase comes in the Sunday brick.

For the Sunday brick, ride 1 hour, 30 minutes and run 30 minutes. Similar to Week 3, this is a negative-split workout. If you ride and run an out-and-back course, the time it takes you to return is slightly faster than the time it took you to go out. This week, go out at intensity Zones 1 to 2 and return at intensity Zones 2 to 3. Learning to control pace early in workouts and races is key to success. Practice hydrating and fueling during this brick.

Week 7

Bike

The Monday bike ride remains a form workout, preceding a strength training session. The Wednesday ride changes. If you have been strength training for the first 6 weeks, it is time to reduce strength training sessions to a maintenance mode. This means strength training once per week on Monday. The Wednesday workout becomes an hour of cycling.

The Sunday long ride holds at 2 hours, 30 minutes to 3 hours, but intensity again increases in this training block. Within a ride that includes intensity Zones 1 to 5a, accumulate 20 to 30 minutes of time in Zones 4 to 5a during the entire ride. If possible, ride a course similar in profile to the course you will ride on race day. Remember to hydrate and fuel during the ride.

Run

The weekday run pattern remains similar to that in previous non-rest weeks. One change is that the length of the Thursday run goes to 30 to 45 minutes. The second change is that the intensity range of the Saturday run includes Zones 1 to 5a. Within the long run, accumulate about 20 minutes of time in Zones 4 to 5a.

Week 8

Bike
The bike pattern for Week 8 is the same as for Week 7. The only change is in the amount of time accumulated during the long ride in Zones 4 to 5a. Accumulate 30 to 45 minutes of time in Zones 4 to 5a during the entire ride.

Run
The weekday run pattern for Week 8 remains the same as for Week 7. However, the long run includes some intervals this week. After a warm-up mostly in Zones 1 to 2, do four to six intervals that are 5 minutes long. Run the intervals in Zones 4 to 5a. Keep in mind that it takes some time for your heart rate to respond to the pace. Begin timing the interval as soon as you begin running in Zones 4 to 5a. After each work interval, jog easy for 2 minutes, getting your heart rate back into Zone 1.

Week 9
The workout pattern for the rest week, Week 9, is the same as for Week 6. Similar to Week 6, the Sunday brick remains a ride of 1 hour, 30 minutes and a run of 30 minutes. As in Week 6, this is a negative-split workout. If you ride and run an out-and-back course, the time it takes to return will be slightly faster than the time it took to go out. This week, go out at intensity Zones 1 to 2 and return at intensity Zones 4 to 5a. This is your race day pace. Learn to pace yourself during the entire workout so you do not "blow up" before the end.

Week 10
This week begins the gentle tapering to race day. Notice the Monday workouts remain the same as in past weeks; however, Tuesday no longer has a scheduled run. Wednesday keeps an hour of form riding on the bike. Thursday keeps a swim and a run, but run time is limited to 30 minutes.

Saturday can be a race simulation day, when you swim, bike, and run in close succession. Or, you can do the swim separate from the brick. In the case of the brick, it is a negative-split effort in both sports. Ride 2 hours and run 45 minutes. In both cases, go out at Zones 1 to 2 intensity and bring it home at Zones 4 to 5a intensity. This is a great time to do a dress rehearsal for race day. Wear exactly what you plan to wear on race day, and simulate your fueling and hydrating as well as pace.

Sunday is an easy, Zone 1 recovery spin on the bike.

Week 11

As always, Monday begins with form work on the bike. If you are still strength training, lighten the weights or eliminate strength training altogether. Wednesday's cycling time is reduced to 45 minutes. Keep the Thursday swim on the lower end of repetitions in the main set. On Saturday, you'll swim and run. Within a run that is mostly at Zones 1 to 2 intensity, include four repeats of 90 seconds, ramping up speed to Zones 4 to 5a. Take 3 minutes of easy recovery between each 90-second repeat.

On Sunday, begin your 1 hour, 30 minute ride, with 20 minutes in Zones 1 and 2. Then do three repeats of 10 minutes in Zones 4 to 5a, 10 minutes in Zones 1 to 2. Spin for 10 minutes in Zone 1 at the end of the workout.

Week 12+

Yahoo, race week! Monday is a short, 30-minute run with two repeats, 90 seconds each. For each repeat, ramp up your speed to Zones 4 to 5a. Know that your heart rate will take a good deal of the 90 seconds to respond. Tuesday and Thursday are swims. Keep them short, aiming for the low end of the number of repeats. Wednesday is a very short brick, just to iron out any last-minute wrinkles. Ride for 30 minutes, immediately followed by a 15-minute run. Include a couple of 20- to 30-second accelerations within each sport. Friday is a day off, and Saturday is a very short bike ride for the purpose of checking your equipment.

Sunday is race day. To reduce anxiety, arrive at the race site with plenty of time to spare. Plan to conduct each sport within the event in a negative-split manner. Begin more slowly than you think you need to and make the second half a bit faster. Fuel and hydrate at regular intervals, setting your watch's beeper to remind you if necessary.

If your race is on Saturday, move the day off to Thursday and the bike gear check to Friday. Eliminate the Thursday swim. In this case, Sunday can be a day off or you can take an easy ride or walk.

Table 7.1 Fit Beginner Plan for an Olympic Distance Triathlon

Week	Monday	Tuesday	Wednesday	Thursday
1	Bike 30 min. at 90 rpm Strength AA 30 minutes	Swim Workout 1 Run 30 min. Zone 1	Bike 30 min. spin-ups Strength AA 30 min.	Swim Workout 2
2	Bike 30 min. at 90 rpm Strength AA 30 min.	Swim: Workout 1 Run 30 min. Zone 1	Bike 30 min. spin-ups Strength AA 30 min.	Swim Workout 2
3	Day off	Swim Workout 1 Run 30 min. Zone 1	Bike 30 min. at 90 rpm Strength AA 30 min.	BRICK Bike 30 min., Run 45 min. Zones 1–2 Include 20–30 sec. accels
4	Bike 30 min. at 90 rpm Strength SM 30 min.	Swim Workout 1 Run 30 min. Zones 1–2	Bike 30 min. with ILT work Strength SM 30 min.	Swim Workout 2 Run 20–30 min. Count cadence Zones 1–2
5	Bike 30 min. at 90 rpm Strength SM 30 min.	Swim Workout 1 Run 30 min. Zones 1–2	Bike 30 min. with ILT work Strength SM 30 min.	Swim Workout 2 Run 20–30 min. Count cadence Zones 1–2
6	Day off	Swim Workout 1 Run 30 min. Cadence Zones 1–2	Bike 30 min. at 90 rpm Strength SM 30 min.	BRICK Bike 30 min. Run 45 min. Zones 1–2 Include 20–30 sec. accels
7	Bike 30 min. spin-ups Strength SM 30 min.	Swim Workout 1 Run 30 min. Zones 1–2	Bike 1 hr. at 90 rpm	Swim Workout 2 Run 30–45 min. Count cadence Zones 1–2
8	Bike 30 min. spin-ups Strength SM 30 min.	Swim Workout 1 Run 30 min. Zones 1–2	Bike 1 hr. at 90 rpm	Swim Workout 2 Run 30–45 min. Count cadence Zones 1–2

For the week after the event, try to make recovery a priority. Work out only if you feel like it and keep the intensity in Zones 1 to 2. Wait until Wednesday or later in the week to run.

Friday	Saturday	Sunday	Weekly Totals
Day off	Run 45 min. Cadence Zones 1–2	Bike 2–2.5 hr. Rolling course Zones 1 to 2	6 hr., 15 min.– 6 hr., 45 min.
Day off	Swim Workout 3 Run 1 hr. Cadence Zones 1–2	Bike 2–2.5 hr. Rolling course Zones 1–2	6 hr., 15 min.– 6 hr., 45 min.
Day off	Swim Workout 3	BRICK Bike 1 hr., Run 15 min. In both sports, travel an out-and-back course. Go out in Zone 1 and come back in Zone 2. This is negative-split—the trip back should be slightly faster than the trip out.	5 hr., 15 min.
Day off	Swim Workout 3 Run 1 hr. Zones 1–3 Accumulate 20–30 min. in Zone 3	Bike 2.5–3 hr. Rolling course Zones 1–3 Accumulate 20–30 min. in Zone 3	7 hr., 35 min.– 8 hr., 30 min.
Day off	Swim Workout 3 Run 1 hr., 15 min. Warm up in Zones 1–2, do 4–6 repeats of 5 min. working your intensity—Zone 3 and holding to the end of the interval. Take 2 min. of easy jogging between each set. Cool down.	Bike 2.5–3 hr. Rolling course Zones 1–3 Accumulate 30–45 min. in Zone 3	7 hr., 50 min.– 8 hr., 45 min.
Day off	Swim Workout 3	BRICK Bike 1.5 hr., Run 30 min. Both sports are negative-split. Travel an out-and-back course. Go out in Zones 1–2 and come back in Zones 2–3.	5 hr., 45 min.
Day off	Swim Workout 3 Run 60–75 min. Zones 1–5a. Mostly Zones 1–2, accumulate 20 min. in Zones 4–5a.	Bike 2.5–3 hr. Rolling/hilly course Zones 1–5a Accumulate 20–30 min. in Zones 4–5a	8 hr., 15 min.– 10 hr.
Day off	Swim Workout 3 Run 60–75 min. Warm up in Zones 1–2, do 4–6 repeats of 5 min. working your intensity—Zones 4–5a and holding intensity there to the end of the interval. Take 2 min. of easy jogging between each set. Cool down.	Bike 2.5–3 hr. Rolling/hilly course Zones 1–5a. Accumulate 30–45 min. in Zones 4–5a	8 hr., 15 min.– 10 hr.

Continued next page

Week	Monday	Tuesday	Wednesday	Thursday
9	Day off	**Swim** Workout 1 **Run** 30 min. Cadence Zones 1–2	**Bike** 30 min. at 90 rpm **Strength** SM 30 min.	**BRICK Bike** 30 min., **Run** 45 min. Zones 1–2 Include 20–30 sec. accels
10	**Bike** 30 min. with ILT work **Strength** SM 30 min.	**Swim** Workout 1	**Bike** 1 hr. at 90 rpm	**Swim** Workout 2 **Run** 20–30 min. Count cadence Zones 1–2
11	**Bike** 30 min. with ILT work **Strength** SM 30 min. Lighter weights **OR** day off	**Swim** Workout 1	**Bike** 45 min. at 90 rpm	**Swim** Workout 2 **Run** 20–30 min. Count cadence Zones 1–2
12	**Run** 30 min. Include 2 x 90 sec. at race pace	**Swim** Workout 1	**BRICK Bike** 30 min. 4 x 30 sec. accels (1 min, 30 sec. RI) **Run** 10 min. 2 x 30 sec. accels (1 min., 30 sec. RI) Zones 1–2	**Swim** Workout 2 (Keep it short today)

Friday	Saturday	Sunday	Weekly Totals
Day off	Swim Workout 3	BRICK Bike 1.5 hr., Run 30 min. Both sports are negative-splits. Travel an out-and-back course. Go out in Zones 1–2 and come back in Zones 4–5a.	5 hr., 45 min.
Day off	Swim Workout 3 BRICK Bike 2 hr., Run 45 min. Both sports are negative-splits. Travel an out-and-back course. Go out in Zones 1–2 and come back in Zones 4–5a.	Bike 1 hr very easy Zone 1	8 hr.
Day off	Swim Workout 3 Run 45 min. Mostly Zones 1–2; include 4 x 90 sec. gently accelerating to Zones 4–5a intensity. Do 3 min. of easy jogging between each acceleration.	Bike 1.5 hr. Warm up in Zones 1–2 for 20 min., then do 4 repeats of (10 min. building intensity into Zones 4–5a range, then 10 min. of easy spinning in Zones 1–2). Cool down for 10 min. in Zone 1.	6 hr., 15 min.
Day off	Bike 30 min. Mostly easy, run through your gears.	Race Race as you have been training, negative-splits.	2 hr., 45 min. + race time

Chapter 8

Unfit Individuals on a Team
Beginner Plans for a Sprint Distance Triathlon

People with a sense of challenge realize that they'll never achieve peak creativity
or experience joy unless they take some risks.
—Source unknown

Let's face it, every good triathlete must experience the beginning of his or her fitness journey. No one begins life with the ability to complete a triathlon. Before starting any fitness program, dormant athletes are, to be honest, unfit. I struggled with using the word "unfit," because it seemed mean-spirited. I kept the word, however, because it isn't intended to be mean; rather it is intended to designate a current lack of fitness.

That current lack of fitness keeps some people from believing they can ever participate in a triathlon. If you are one of the nonbelievers, I'm here to convince you otherwise. I believe that beginning with very limited fitness—what some would consider a total lack of fitness—by the end of 6 weeks of training you can be a member of a triathlon team, completing a sprint distance race for the first time. Don't believe it's possible? Read on.

Goal

Complete one event of a sprint distance triathlon at the end of 6 weeks of preparation. You are either the swimmer, completing approximately 500 yards (or meters) of swimming; the cyclist, riding some 15 miles; or the runner, covering around 3.1 miles.

Profiles

This chapter provides a 6-week training plan for each team member. No, you don't have to recruit only unfit people to your team. However, there is something magical about making a pact with your unfit buddies. You begin your quest in the spirit of "We're going to get back into shape. We're going to start our fitness comeback by doing a sprint distance triathlon as a team. Each of us needs to train three times per week, that's all, for 6 weeks. Are ya in?"

Swimmer

As the team swimmer, you are currently capable of swimming 25 yards. (For the rest of the text, you can interchange yards and meters.) Distances much beyond 25 yards leave you gasping for air. You have no endurance ... yet. Have a look at Table 8.1 to see how the plan gently builds endurance. (See table at the end of this chapter.)

Cyclist

Your bike has been stored in the garage for a while. Okay, a long while. Neighborhood kids have written, "I want to go for a spin" in the dust on your top tube. Given the right motivation, like a team triathlon, you believe that you can ride 30 minutes, three times in the first week of training. Table 8.2 displays a plan to build your cycling endurance to between 75 and 90 minutes. (See table at the end of this chapter.) This endurance level is plenty for you to complete 15 miles on race day successfully.

Runner

Perhaps you are a former runner? Or maybe you have always wanted to run a 5K race (3.1 miles) but did not know how to begin, and your motivation for running any event has been squelched by the lack of a goal. Now you have a clear goal. You are *the runner* for your triathlon team. Your teammates are depending on you.

Because you want to minimize your risk of injury, you aim to begin your fitness journey with a program that mixes running and walking. On the first day of training, you begin the workout by walking 10 minutes, then you do five repeats of running for a minute and walking for a minute. Yes, that's all for the first day. In just 6 weeks, you will have the fitness to run or run/walk 3.1 miles. Table 8.3 outlines your journey. (See table at the end of this chapter.) Look like a plan you can accomplish? Yes? Great!

The Plan

Most of your workout time is spent at Zones 1 and 2 intensity. (See Chapter 3 for further information on intensity levels.) If you have a heart rate monitor and know your training zones, that's great. Many currently hibernating athletes do not have heart rate monitors and will use rating of perceived exertion (RPE) for the exercise program.

At some point during the training weeks, your team should have a meeting and talk about the logistics on race day. Can you view the course in advance? Where will the transition area be located? Does the exchange between team members involve a wristband or an ankle timing chip? These are all good items to discuss prior to race day.

All of the plans leading to race day in this chapter show workouts on Tuesday, Thursday, and Saturday. If it's more convenient for you to work out on Monday, Wednesday, and Friday, you can move the workouts accordingly.

Swimmer

Week 1
The training plan in Table 8.1 shows your first workout on Tuesday of Week 1. The Tuesday workout assignment is to swim twenty repeats of 25 yards (20 x 25), resting 20 seconds (20 sec. RI) between each

repeat. Swim all repeats at an RPE in Zones 1 and 2. Note how much time it takes you to complete the entire set from start to finish. This time will improve by the end of the program.

While swimming repeats, some people have a tough time keeping track of the number of repeats they have completed. "Now, was that number 11 or number 13?" One method for keeping track is to take ten pennies to the pool with you and place them next to your water bottle. Each time you complete two repeats of 25 yards (placing you back at your starting point), move one penny from one side of your water bottle to the other side. When you have moved all the pennies from one side to the other, the set is finished.

The set on Thursday of Week 1 is five rounds of 4 x 25 yards, resting 10 seconds between each 25. The rest is shorter between each 25, but you get an extra minute of rest after each set of four (1 minute between rounds). Swim 4 x 25 (10 seconds of rest between each one), rest 1 minute after number four, swim 4 x 25 (10 seconds of rest between each one), rest 1 minute after number four, and so on until you swim five rounds. All swims are at RPE Zones 1 and 2.

The Saturday swim of Week 1 is similar to the Tuesday workout, in that you swim 20 x 25 yards, resting at 20-second intervals. But the odd-numbered ones (1, 3, 5, 7...) are easy, Zone 1 intensity. The even-numbered ones (2, 4, 6, 8...) are completed so that you swim faster at the end of the 25 yards than you did at the beginning. You build speed throughout the 25 yards.

Week 2

The Tuesday workout this week is similar to last week's, in that you swim 20 x 25 yards. However, this week there is less rest between each one—only 15 seconds. The Thursday workout is two or three rounds, your choice, of four repeats of 50 yards, resting 20 seconds between each 50. After completing the first round of 4 x 50, rest an extra minute before heading into the next round. Be sure to pace yourself so you have enough energy to swim strong on the last ones.

The Saturday swim is nine or ten repeats of 50 yards, with 30 seconds of rest between each one. There is plenty of rest, so you can swim easy on the odd-numbered 50s and build your speed throughout the even-numbered 50s. Finish each even-numbered 50 faster than you began.

Week 3

The pattern on Tuesday remains the same, 20 x 25 yards. This week, the rest is only 10 seconds between each 25. The Thursday workout is two rounds of four repeats of 75 yards, resting 20 seconds between each 75. After completing the first round of 4 x 75, rest an extra minute before heading into the next round. The Saturday swim this week is a repeat of last week's. Swim nine or ten repeats of 50 yards, resting 30 seconds between each one. There is plenty of rest, so once again you can swim easy on the odd-numbered 50s and build your speed throughout the even-numbered 50s. Finish each even-numbered 50 faster than you began.

Week 4

The pattern on Tuesday remains the same, 20 x 25 yards. This week, the rest is only 5 seconds between each 25! The Thursday workout is five repeats of 100 yards, resting 20 seconds between each 100. The Saturday swim is two rounds of four repeats of 75 yards, resting 30 seconds between each 75. Odd-numbered 75s are easy, and during the even-numbered 75s you will build speed throughout the entire 75 yards. After completing the first round of 4 x 75, rest an extra minute before heading into the next round.

Week 5

Remember Week 1, when you noted the time it took you to complete 20 x 25 yards, with 20-second rest intervals? The Tuesday workout is a repeat of that first workout, so you can see the progress you have made. Good job!

The Thursday workout this week is your first 500-yard, nonstop swim. Swim at the same pace you have used in other workouts, in Zones 1 and 2. Relax and try to swim with the least amount of effort possible.

The Saturday workout is 5 x 100 yards, resting 1 minute between each 100 yards. The goal for this workout is to swim each 100 yards faster than the previous one. This means you need to concentrate on swimming the first one very, very easy and gently build your speed from there.

Week 6

Race week has finally arrived. It is important to rest this week, so don't be tempted to swim more than shown in the plan. The Tuesday workout is only ten repeats of 25 yards, with 20-second rest intervals. The odd-numbered 25s are easy and the even-numbered 25s build speed throughout. The Thursday workout is a repeat of Tuesday's, or take the day off and rest.

Although the plan shows Saturday as race day, a race on Sunday does not change the plan layout. Plan to swim the race exactly as you have completed many workouts. Begin slower than you think you should and build speed throughout the entire 500-yard swim.

Cyclist

Week 1

Table 8.2 displays your 6-week plan to race day. The Tuesday workout in Week 1 begins with a 30-minute ride at Zones 1 to 2 intensity, on a flat course, and pedaling at 90 revolutions per minute. If you don't have a cadence sensor as part of your bicycle computer, you can count the number of times your right leg reaches the bottom of the pedal stroke in 15 seconds. The number should be 22 or higher.

The Thursday ride is 30 minutes long, mostly at Zones 1 and 2 intensity. At each 5-minute mark (0:05, 0:10, 0:15…), pedal for 30 seconds using primarily your right leg, then 30 seconds using primarily your left leg. At the top of the pedal stroke, drive your knee and toes forward. As your foot begins the downward motion, apply pressure to the pedal as if you were scraping mud off your foot on the curb of a street. As your foot moves to the back of the pedal stroke, lift and unweight your foot and prepare to drive your knee and toes forward again. If you have a "dead spot" in your pedal stroke, it becomes obvious immediately during this drill. Meanwhile, the nonworking leg puts out minimal effort.

On Saturday, ride for 30 minutes at Zones 1 to 2 intensity on a flat course.

Week 2

The Tuesday workout is a repeat of last week's, 30 minutes in Zones 1 to 2 at a cadence of 90 rpm. The Thursday ride increases to 45 minutes in Zones 1 to 2, keeping the 30-second right leg, 30-second left leg drill at each 5-minute mark. The Saturday ride increases to 45 minutes at Zones 1 to 2 intensity.

Week 3

The workouts in Week 3 are the same as for Week 2 on Tuesday and Thursday. The Saturday ride increases to 60 minutes on a gently rolling course: Notice that you can increase the intensity to Zone 3. Your goal is not to maximize Zone 3 time, rather to allow it to increase as you ride up the hills.

Week 4

The Tuesday workout changes to include accelerations this week. Within your 30-minute ride, include four to six accelerations, taking 1 minute, 30 seconds' recovery between each one. Accelerations (accels) are not all-out sprints, but rather a gentle building of speed throughout the 30 seconds.

The Thursday ride can be 45 to 60 minutes long, your choice. Also, move the single-leg drills to each 10-minute mark. For Saturday, try to ride a course similar to the course you will ride on race day. The ride can be 60 to 75 minutes long.

Week 5

The Tuesday and Thursday workouts remain the same as in Week 4. On Saturday, increase your ride time to between 75 and 90 minutes.

Week 6

Warning, warning! Do not be tempted to do more workouts this week. Your race day performance will suffer if you do. For this reason, the Thursday workout becomes optional. If you have a lot going on in your life, it is better to rest and be fresh for the race. On race day, ride the event at the same intensity you have practiced in workouts. Plan to finish the distance stronger than you began. This means starting a little easier than you think you should. Go fast and have fun!

Runner

Of the three triathlon sports, running typically carries the greatest risk for injury. To minimize your risk of injury, it is important that you have appropriate running shoes. No, the tennies you have worn every week-end for the past year will not work. Go to a good running gear store and ask one of the store experts for help in finding the right shoe for you.

Another strategy you will use to minimize injury risk is a run/walk strategy. By gently alternating running and walking, you condition your tendons, ligaments, and muscles to adapt slowly to the stress of running. The plan builds your running time so that you can run the entire event on race day, if you choose. Some of you may want to run/walk on race day and that is fine, too.

All workouts, including race day, are at Zones 1 and 2 intensity. Allow yourself to do some workouts entirely in Zone 1.

Week 1

On Tuesday, begin your workout by walking for 10 minutes. After 10 minutes, run or jog for 1 minute, then walk for another minute. Repeat the 1-minute run, 1-minute walk five times. The Thursday workout is similar to Tuesday's, except that you begin by walking for 6 minutes before alternating 1-minute run segments with 1-minute walking segments. Repeat the run/walk pattern seven times.

The Saturday workout is slightly longer at 30 minutes. Begin the session by walking 10 minutes before completing ten repeats of the 1-minute run, 1-minute walk pattern.

Week 2

The Tuesday workout is five repetitions of walking for 2 minutes, then running for 2 minutes. On Thursday, the walking segment decreases to 1 minute. Walk 1 minute and run for 2 minutes, repeating the pattern seven times. The Saturday workout moves to six repetitions of walking for 2 minutes and running for 3 minutes. Good job!

Week 3

As you continue to build your running time, on Tuesday complete four repeats of walking 1 minute and running 4 minutes. Thursday begins with a 2-minute walk before three repeats of walking 1 minute and running 5 minutes. Saturday begins with a 9-minute walk before you complete three repeats of 1 minute of walking and 6 minutes of running.

Week 4

On Tuesday, complete two repeats of 2 minutes of walking and 8 minutes of running. Thursday is two repeats of 1 minute of walking and 9 minutes of running. Saturday is three repeats of 2 minutes of walking and 8 minutes of running.

Week 5

Tuesday begins with a 5-minute walk, then 15 minutes of continuous running. On Thursday, you can run for 20 minutes continuously or run for most of the 20 minutes, including 30-second walking breaks at each 5-minute mark. On Saturday you can run for 30 minutes or complete three repeats of running for 9 minutes and walking 1 minute.

Week 6

Race week has finally arrived! Don't be tempted to work out any more than shown in the plan. Your goal is to feel rested for race day. On Tuesday, complete four repeats of walking for a minute and running for 4 minutes. On Thursday, run for 10 minutes or take the day off. On race day, run or run/walk the 3.1 miles at the same intensity you have used in training.

Table 8.1 Unfit Beginner Sprint Distance Plan for Teams—Swimmer

Week	Monday	Tuesday	Wednesday	Thursday
1	Day off	Swim 20 x 25 (20 sec. RI) Zones 1–2 Get your time	Day off	Swim 4 x 25 (10 sec. RI) Repeat 5 rounds, 1-min. RI between rounds. Zones 1–2
2	Day off	Swim 20 x 25 (15 sec. RI) Zones 1–2	Day off	Swim 4 x 50 (20 sec. RI) Repeat 2–3 rounds, 1-min. RI between rounds. Zones 1–2
3	Day off	Swim 20 x 25 (10 sec. RI) Zones 1–2	Day off	Swim 4 x 75 (20 sec. RI) Repeat 2 rounds, 1-min. RI between rounds. Zones 1–2
4	Day off	Swim 20 x 25 (5 sec. RI) Zones 1–2	Day off	Swim 5 x 100 (20 sec. RI) Zones 1–2
5	Day off	Swim 20 x 25 (20 sec. RI) Zones 1–2 Get your time	Day off	Swim 500 steady Zones 1–2
6	Day off	Swim 10 x 25 (10 sec. RI) Odds EZ Evens, build to race pace	Day off	Swim 10 x 25 (10 sec. RI) Odds EZ Evens, build to race pace OR take the day off

Table 8.2 Unfit Beginner Sprint Distance Plan for Teams—Cyclist

Week	Monday	Tuesday	Wednesday
1	Day off	Bike 30 min. at 90 rpm, flat course Zones 1–2	Day off
2	Day off	Bike 30 min. at 90 rpm, flat course Zones 1–2	Day off
3	Day off	Bike 30 min. at 90 rpm, flat course Zones 1–2	Day off
4	Day off	Bike 30 min. in mostly Zones 1–2 Include 4–6 x 30 sec. accels (1 min., 30 sec. RI)	Day off
5	Day off	Bike 30 min. in mostly Zones 1–2 Include 4–6 x 30 sec. accels (1 min., 30 sec. RI)	Day off
6	Day off	Bike 30 min. in mostly Zones 1–2 Include 4–6 x 30 sec. accels (1 min., 30 sec. RI)	Day off

Friday	Saturday	Sunday
Day off	**Swim** 20 x 25 (20 sec. RI) Odds EZ Evens, build speed	Day off
Day off	**Swim** 9–10 x 50 (30 sec. RI) Odds EZ Evens, build speed	Day off
Day off	**Swim** 9–10 x 50 (20 sec. RI) Odds EZ Evens, build speed	Day off
Day off	**Swim** 4 x 75 (30 sec. RI) Repeat 2 rounds, 1 min. RI between rounds. Odds EZ; Evens, build speed	Day off
Day off	**Swim** 5 x 100 (1 min. RI) Make each 100 faster than the previous one.	Day off
Day off	Race **Swim** 500	Day off

Thursday	Friday	Saturday	Sunday
Bike 30 min. At each 5-min. mark, pedal 30 sec. right leg, 30 sec. left leg. Zones 1–2	Day off	**Bike** 30 min. Flat course Zones 1–2	Day off
Bike 45 min. At each 5-min. mark, pedal 30 sec. right leg, 30 sec. left leg. Zones 1–2	Day off	**Bike** 45 min. Flat course Zones 1–2	Day off
Bike 45 min. At each 5-min. mark, pedal 30 sec. right leg, 30 sec. left leg. Zones 1–2	Day off	**Bike** 60 min. Flat course Zones 1–3	Day off
Bike 45–60 min. At each 10-min. mark, pedal 30 sec. right leg, 30 sec. left leg. Zones 1–2	Day off	**Bike** 60–75 min. Course similar to the racecourse. Zones 1–3	Day off
Bike 45–60 min. At each 10-min. mark, pedal 30 sec. right leg, 30 sec. left leg. Zones 1–2	Day off	**Bike** 75–90 min. Course similar to the racecourse. Zones 1–3	Day off
Bike 30 min. At each 5-min. mark, pedal 30 sec. right leg, 30 sec. left leg. Zones 1–2 OR Take the day off	Day off	Race **Bike** 15 miles	Day off

Table 8.3 Unfit Beginner Sprint Distance Plan for Teams—Runner

Week	Monday	Tuesday	Wednesday	Thursday
1	Day off	Run/Walk 20 min.: Walk 10 min., then 5 x (run 1 min., walk 1 min.) Zones 1–2	Day off	Run/Walk 20 min.: Walk 6 min., then 7 x (run 1 min., walk 1 min.) Zones 1–2
2	Day off	Run/Walk 20 min.: 5 x (walk 2 min., run 2 min.) Zones 1–2	Day off	Run/Walk 21 min.: 7 x (walk 1 min., run 2 min.) Zones 1–2
3	Day off	Run/Walk 20 min.: 4 x (walk 1 min., run 4 min.) Zones 1–2	Day off	Run/Walk 20 min.: Walk 2 min., then 3 x (walk 1 min., run 5 min.) Zones 1–2
4	Day off	Run/Walk 20 min.: 2 x (walk 2 min., run 8 min.) Zones 1–2	Day off	Run/Walk 20 min.: 2 x (walk 1 min., run 9 min.) Zones 1–2
5	Day off	Run/Walk 20 min.: Walk 5 min., then run 15 min. Zones 1–2	Day off	Run 20 min. steady Zones 1–2 **Optional:** Walk 30 sec. at each 5-min. mark
6	Day off	Run/Walk 20 min.: 4 x (walk 1 min., run 4 min.) Zones 1–2	Day off	Run 10 min. steady Zones 1–2 **OR** Take the day off

Friday	Saturday	Sunday
Day off	**Run/Walk** 30 min.: Walk 10 min., then 10 x (run 1 min., walk 1 min.) Zones 1–2	Day off
Day off	**Run/Walk** 30 min.: 6 x (walk 2 min., run 3 min.) Zones 1–2	Day off
Day off	**Run/Walk** 30 min.: Walk 9 min., then 3 x (walk 1 min., run 6 min.) Zones 1–2	Day off
Day off	**Run/Walk** 30 min.: 3 x (walk 2 min., run 8 min.) Zones 1–2	Day off
Day off	**Run/Walk** 30 min.: 3 x (walk 1 min., run 9 min.) Zones 1–2 **Optional:** Run 30 min. steady	Day off
Day off	**Race** **Run** or **Run/Walk** 3.1 miles	Day off

Chapter 9

Fit Individuals on a Team
Beginner Plans for a Sprint Distance Triathlon

*You control your future, your destiny. What you think about
comes about. By recording your dreams and goals on paper,
you set in motion the process of becoming the person
you most want to be. Put your future in good hands: your own.*
—Mark Victor Hansen

What is a "fit beginner"? For the purposes of this chapter, fit beginners
are athletes who stay in good aerobic shape. They work out three to four
times per week on their own, at a gym or a health club. While they have
good aerobic fitness, their speed is dusty, covered by a few cobwebs.
Wouldn't it be fun to complete a sprint distance triathlon with your buddies? How about dusting off the speed workouts and adding some spice
to your routine? If spice sounds fun, read on.

Goal
Complete one event of a sprint distance triathlon at the end of 6 weeks
of preparation. You are either the swimmer, completing approximately

500 yards (or meters) of swimming; the cyclist, riding some 15 miles; or the runner, covering around 3.1 miles.

Profiles

This chapter provides a 6-week training plan for each team member. If one of your team members is less fit than described in the profiles, see Chapter 8. Plans for faster, experienced athletes are not covered in this book.

Swimmer

As the team swimmer, you are currently capable of swimming 500 yards nonstop. (For the rest of the text, you can interchange yards and meters.) In your current swimming routine, you typically just get in the pool and swim laps, with no regard for pace. It would be nice, however, to improve your speed.

Cyclist

You are currently riding three times per week. On 2 weekdays, you ride for 45 to 60 minutes. These rides can be in organized, indoor cycling workouts or on your own. At least one of your rides is an hour to an hour-and-a-half long, usually outdoors.

Runner

You usually run 3 days per week. Two days are 20- to 30-minute sessions, with one longer run between 30 and 45 minutes. You tend to run the same routes because they are convenient. Most of the time, you run at the same pace because you are not training for a race and do not know why or how to change the routine. An easy-to-follow plan to change your routine sounds interesting.

The Plan

Since you are already in good aerobic shape, you have a good base of fitness. For each of the three sports, three different workouts are shown in the plans. If you want to add a fourth workout on your own, keep it easy. An easy workout is recommended, rather than an additional fast or speed-work session. (To gauge intensity, see Chapter 3 for foundation instructions.) The cyclist and runner plans in this chapter reference training zones. The swimming plan uses training zones in addition to pace.

At some point during the training weeks, your team needs to have a meeting and talk about the logistics for race day. Can you view the course in advance? Where is the transition area located? Does the exchange between team members involve a wristband or an ankle timing chip? These are all good items to discuss prior to race day.

All of the plans leading to race day in this chapter show workouts on Tuesday, Thursday, and Saturday. If it is more convenient for you to work out on Monday, Wednesday, and Friday, you can move the workouts accordingly.

Swimmer

Week 1

The plan in Table 9.1 shows your first workout on Tuesday of Week 1. (See table at the end of this chapter.) The Tuesday workout assignment is to complete a warm-up of 100 to 300 yards, then swim a 500-yard time trial (yards and meters can be used interchangeably throughout the text). Your goal is to swim the entire distance as fast as possible. Be careful not to sprint the first 50 yards and slowly fade the remaining 450. Ideally, the last 250 yards of the time trial will be faster than the first 250 yards. This strategy is called "negative-split." Note your time for the swim and cool down with easy swimming for 100 to 300 yards. Cool-down yards are not specified in the plan. However, after each main set, you should spend some 100 to 300 yards swimming easy and stretching.

The average pace you held for that time trial is called your "T-Pace" within this plan. For example, if your 500 time is 10 minutes, 25 seconds, then your T-Pace is 2 minutes, 5 seconds per 100 yards or 1 minute, 2.5 seconds for 50 yards. You will use your T-Pace and the clock to help you improve your swimming speed. Some pools have a pace clock on the wall, while others do not. You may have to use your own waterproof sports watch to time swimming intervals.

On Thursday of Week 1, the workout is "Warm up, then 5–6 x (50 kick, 50 swim), 10–15 sec. RI after each swim, Zones 1–2." For the remainder of the plan, the warm-up yardage is left up to you. Depending on your swimming ability and the time you have available to work out, warm up between 100 and 500 yards before the main set of each workout.

After your warm-up on Thursday, complete five or six repeats of 50 yards of kicking (with or without a kickboard), immediately followed by 50 yards of swimming. The intensity of the kick and the swim is in Zones 1 to 2. It should feel easier than your T-Pace. After each 50-yard swim, rest only 10 to 15 seconds before beginning the next 50-yard kick, immediately followed by a 50-yard swim. The 10 to 15 seconds of rest following each swim is called your rest interval, designated by "RI" on the chart.

The Saturday swim of Week 1 utilizes your T-Pace for 50 yards. After the warm-up, swim six to eight repeats of 50 yards as fast as you can. If your time per 50 gets slower, don't worry—just swim each 50 as fast as possible. The rest between each 50 may vary slightly, because this work-out utilized a set swim interval (SI). The swim interval is your T-Pace plus 1 minute. Using the sample swimmer's time of 1 minute, 2.5 seconds, the swim interval would be 2 minutes, 2.5 seconds. Round off to a swim interval of 2 minutes. Every time the pace clock hits the 2-minute mark, begin another fast 50 swim. After completing all of the fast 50s, be sure to cool down.

Week 2

The Tuesday workout this week is a warm-up followed by five to six repeats of 100 yards. The swim interval (SI) is T-Pace plus 15 seconds. Our sample swimmer would use a swim interval 2 minutes, 5 seconds plus 15 seconds or 2 minutes, 20 seconds. The rest between swims is much shorter than you had on Saturday. Your swim pace for Tuesday is your T-Pace or slightly faster by 1 to 3 seconds. Our sample swimmer would swim each 100 repeat between a pace of 2 minutes, 2 seconds and 2 min-utes, 5 seconds. The pace should feel challenging, but not impossible. Controlling the pace and rest interval is the secret of this workout.

The Thursday workout is very similar to that in Week 1, except the kick and swim distance is 75 yards instead of 50 yards. The rest interval remains 15 seconds after each swim.

The Saturday workout this week uses the same swim interval of last week, but the way you swim each 50 is slightly different. The chart notes, "swim 6 x 50 descend." This means each 50-yard swim is faster than the previous one. Watch the clock and control your pace so the first 50 is the slowest and the last 50 is the fastest. Our sample athlete swims these on the 2-minute swim interval.

After the 50s, rest for a couple of minutes before heading into six to eight repeats of 25 yards as fast as possible. The swim interval is T-Pace plus 1 minute. Our sample swimmer has a 50-yard T-Pace of 1 minute, 2.5 seconds, so 25-yard T-Pace is roughly 31 seconds. The swim interval for this swimmer is 1 minute, 30 seconds. You will have ample rest, so your swims can be very fast. Be sure to cool down with easy swimming after the fast swims.

Week 3

The Tuesday swim is three repeats of 200 yards on a swim interval of T-Pace plus 20 seconds. For our sample swimmer, with a 100-yard T-Pace of 2 minutes, 5 seconds, the 200-yard T-Pace is 4 minutes, 10 seconds. The swim interval for this workout is 4 minutes, 30 seconds. The swim pace is T-Pace or slightly faster. If your pool has a clock on the wall, sneak a peak at the clock to monitor your pace.

The Thursday workout has the same pattern of kicking and swimming. This week, the kick is 25 yards and the swim is 75. For this session, it works well to kick without a kickboard for 25 yards, then go right to swimming 75 yards. When you add your arms after using only your legs to propel yourself, notice how much faster you feel.

On Saturday, swim six repeats of a broken 75 yards. The first 50 yards of the swim is moderate or Zone 3 effort, and the last 25 yards is fast. For this workout, you can choose how to swim the 25 yards. You can swim each one as fast as possible, or swim each one fast—but at the same speed for each one.

Week 4

The Tuesday workout is a pyramid. After warm-up, you will swim increasing distances with increasing rest intervals at Zones 1 to 2 intensity. Your rest interval is 5 seconds per 25 yards of swimming. With rest intervals shown in parentheses, swim 25 (5 seconds), 50 (10 seconds), 75 (15 seconds), 100 (20 seconds), 100 (20 seconds), 75 (15 seconds), 50 (10 seconds), and 25 (5 seconds).

Thursday continues the kick-and-swim format, with three or four repeats of 100 yards of kicking, immediately followed by 100 yards of swimming. Rest 15 seconds following each swim. Intensity is in Zones 1 and 2.

The Saturday workout is warm-up, followed by the main set. The main set includes two repeats of 100 yards at T-Pace, four repeats of 50 yards swum slightly faster than T-Pace, then six repeats of 25 yards going all-out fast. Rest 20 to 30 seconds between each swim. As you progress through the set, you will get more rest time relative to swim time, but swim speed should increase.

Week 5

The Tuesday swim this week is a repeat of Week 2. It is a warm-up, followed by five to six repeats of 100 yards. The swim interval (SI) is T-Pace plus 15 seconds.

The Thursday workout is similar to the Week 3 swim, except you begin the set with 75 yards of swimming, immediately followed by 25 yards of kicking. The kick may feel slow following the 75 swim, but the 75 swim that follows the rest should feel faster.

The Saturday swim is similar to the Week 3 Saturday swim with six repeats of a broken 75 yards. The first 50 yards of the swim is moderate effort and the last 25 yards is fast. This week there is 1 minute of rest between each 75-yard swim, so the 25 is all-out fast swimming.

Week 6

Race week has finally arrived. It is important to rest this week, so don't be tempted to do more swimming than shown on the plan. Keep your warm-up short on Tuesday. Follow the warm-up with a 500-yard steady swim, where the odd-numbered 25s are fast and the even 25s are very easy. Take a short cooldown and get out of the pool.

On Thursday, after warm-up, swim six or eight repeats of 25 yards in which you gently build speed throughout the 25. Rest 30 seconds between swims.

Although the plan shows Saturday as race day, a race on Sunday does not change the plan layout. Plan to swim the race at your fastest average pace. Recall from your Week 1 time trial that you want to swim the last 250 yards slightly faster than the first 250 yards. You want to negative-split the swim.

Cyclist

For the weekday workouts, you can utilize an indoor trainer, a stationary bike, or a cycling class at a gym or health club. For your long ride, try to ride outdoors. Practice good form on the road by staying as far to the right as possible, try to ride a straight line, use your gears to keep your cadence greater than 80 revolutions per minute, and practice drinking while riding a steady, straight line.

Week 1

Table 9.2 displays your 6-week plan to race day. (See table at the end of this chapter.) The Tuesday workout in Week 1 begins with a 30-minute ride at mostly Zones 1 to 2 intensity, on a flat course. After a warm-up, include four or five repeats of 30-second accelerations (accels). An acceleration is an increase in leg speed to near maximum. If your butt begins to bounce off the seat, reduce your leg speed some and hold the high revolutions per minute (rpm) to the end of the 30 seconds. Take 2 minutes, 30 seconds between each acceleration to recover. Relaxed, yet fast, leg speed is the goal.

The Thursday ride is 30 to 45 minutes long. After a good warm-up, include three repeats, 2 minutes long, of fast riding. Your rating of perceived exertion (RPE) or your heart rate is at Zone 5b intensity. This is sustainable, very fast riding. Take 2 minutes between each repeat to recover. During recovery, select an easy gear and spin in Zone 1.

On Saturday, ride between 1 hour and 1 hour, 15 minutes. It is best if you select a course that is similar to the race day course. After a warm-up, include some riding in all intensities from Zones 1 to 5a. During the ride, accumulate 10 to 15 minutes in the range of Zones 4 to 5a. You can use the hills to push for higher intensity, or push your speed on the flats, or do some of both. Be sure to spin easy to cool down at the end. Carry water or a sports drink on this ride and practice drinking on a regular basis—every 15 minutes or so.

Week 2

The Tuesday workout in Week 2 is similar to Week 1, with your total ride time between 30 and 45 minutes. After a warm-up, include four to six repeats of 30-second accelerations (accels). Again, if your butt begins to bounce off the seat, reduce your leg speed some and hold the high revolutions per minute (rpm) to the end of the 30 seconds. Take 2 minutes, 30 seconds between each acceleration to recover.

On Thursday, the workout is at the same intensity as in Week 1, but builds to include another interval. The ride is 30 to 45 minutes long. After a good warm-up, include four repeats, 2 minutes long, of fast riding. Your RPE or your heart rate is at Zone 5b intensity. Take 2 minutes of easy spinning between each fast effort to recover.

For Saturday, ride between 1 hour and 1 hour, 15 minutes. As with last week, it is best if you select a course that is similar to the race day course. After a warm-up, include some riding in all intensities from Zones 1 to 5a. During the ride, accumulate 10 to 15 minutes in the range of Zones 4 to 5a. You can use the hills to push for higher intensity, or push your speed on the flats, or do some of both. Be sure to spin easy to cool down at the end. Carry water or a sports drink on this ride and practice drinking on a regular basis—every 15 minutes or so.

Week 3

The Tuesday workout this week changes. After your warm-up, complete four or five sets of pedaling for 30 seconds using primarily your right leg, then 30 seconds using primarily your left leg, immediately followed by 1 minute of pedaling with both legs at 90 rpm or more. After each segment of pedaling with both legs, go back to isolated leg pedaling until you complete four or five cycles.

For your isolated leg work, at the top of the pedal stroke, drive your knee and toes forward. As your foot begins the downward motion, apply pressure to the pedal as if you were scraping mud off your foot on the curb of a street. As your foot moves to the back of the pedal stroke, lift and unweight your foot and prepare to drive your knee and toes forward again. If you have a "dead spot" in your pedal stroke, it becomes obvious immediately during this drill. Meanwhile, the nonworking leg puts out minimal effort.

The Thursday workout builds on the previous week's pattern. Your total ride this week is around 45 minutes long and includes five repeats of 2 minutes into Zone 5b, after your warm-up.

The Saturday ride also changes this week. While the ride length remains between 1 hour and 1 hour, 15 minutes, this week includes three or four repeats that are 4 minutes long, with 1 minute of recovery between each. When your 4-minute interval begins, gently increase speed until your heart rate reaches Zone 4. Hold intensity steady within Zones 4 to 5a for a duration of 4 minutes. Spin very easy for a minute and begin a new interval.

You will find that during the first interval it takes quite awhile before your heart rate reaches Zone 4. As the intervals progress, you will achieve Zone 4 intensity much sooner than you did during the first one. Be sure to spin easy and cool down after the last interval.

Week 4

The Tuesday workout is a repeat of last week's session, but you will increase the number of sets to five or six. Thursday's workout remains 45 minutes long, with repeats into Zone 5b. But the work interval increases to 3 minutes. Complete three repeats of work and rest.

The Saturday ride holds duration at 1 hour to 1 hour, 15 minutes. After warm-up, complete three or four work intervals that are 5 minutes long, again working in Zones 4 to 5a. Take 3 minutes between each work interval to recover.

Week 5

This week begins with a combination of past Tuesday workouts. After a warm-up, complete four sets of 30 seconds right leg only, 30 seconds left leg only, and 1 minute of spinning with both legs. After completing four sets of the single-leg work, complete four sets of a 30-second acceleration, followed by a 1-minute, 30-second easy spin at 90 rpm or greater.

Thursday's intervals remain 3 minutes long, after your warm-up, riding at speeds that are at Zone 5b intensity. Complete three or four repeats of 3-minute work intervals, followed by 3-minute recovery intervals.

The Saturday ride is only an hour long. After your warm-up, ride 20 minutes steady at Zones 4 to 5a intensity. Leave enough time at the end for a cooldown.

Week 6

Ah, race week. It's time to keep under control and rest this week. Do not be tempted to do more workouts or to attempt greater intensity than shown in the plan for this week. Your race day performance will suffer if you do.

The Tuesday session this week is the same as last week's session. The Thursday ride is only 30 minutes long, with a couple of accelerations included after your warm-up. Run through all your gears during the ride to be certain everything is in working order.

On Saturday, be sure to arrive at the race venue early enough to find a good parking spot and meet your team. Team bikes are usually racked in a special location in the transition area. If possible, do a short warm-up before your segment of the event. If it is not possible to warm up, gently increase your intensity during the first 10 to 15 minutes of the race. Once warmed up, you can race at mostly Zones 4 to 5a intensity and finish the last mile or so at 5b intensity. Be sure to cool down after the race.

Runner

Table 9.3 outlines your running plan. (See table at the end of this chapter.) The general pattern is to work on running economy on Tuesday and muscular endurance on Wednesday. Saturday is the long run that gives you a multifaceted workout. Not only are you building endurance by increasing overall run time, you are also working on sport-specific strength by training on hills. By running at speeds near lactate threshold, you are working on muscular endurance.

Week 1

On Tuesday, begin your workout with a warm-up that is mostly in Zone 1. This workout is meant to be easy. After the warm-up, complete

3 x 20-second accelerations (accels). An acceleration is a gentle building of speed, not an all-out sprint. After each acceleration, return to easy running for 1 minute, 40 seconds before beginning the next acceleration. Relaxed speed is your goal. Going fast should feel easy.

On Thursday, warm up in Zones 1 and 2. Near the end of your run, include a steady 5 minutes at Zones 4 to 5a intensity. Begin timing the 5-minute interval when you begin running at a perceived exertion of Zones 4 to 5a. It may take a minute or more for your heart rate to respond accordingly. Leave enough time for an easy cool-down jog.

The Saturday workout can be between 30 and 45 minutes, depending on your current fitness level. Run on a rolling course. After a warm-up in Zones 1 and 2, vary your intensity from Zone 1 to Zone 5a. During the run, accumulate 5 to 10 minutes in Zones 4 to 5a. This can be accomplished by maintaining a strong and steady pace while running up the hill. This effort allows a gentle and steady rise in your heart. Cap the intensity level at Zone 5a. Be sure to leave enough time for a cooldown.

Week 2

Week 2 training builds on Week 1. The Tuesday workout includes three or four 20-second accelerations. The Thursday workout accumulates between 7 and 10 minutes in Zones 4 to 5a. If you ran 20 minutes on Thursday of last week, run 25 this week. The Saturday run is on a rolling course, accumulating 10 to 15 minutes in Zones 4 to 5a. If you ran 30 minutes last Saturday, run 35 to 40 minutes this week.

Week 3

The Tuesday workout changes slightly, in that the accelerations increase to 30 seconds in length and the recovery interval is shortened to 1 minute, 30 seconds. Complete three or four accelerations. The Thursday workout moves to 30 minutes in length and the intensity increases to Zone 5b. After a good warm-up, complete two intervals that are 3 minutes long. The intervals are run at Zone 5b intensity, which is roughly your 5k race pace. Be careful not to begin too fast and then fade at the end of the interval. Finish each interval faster than you began. Begin timing the interval as soon as you increase pace. It may take awhile for your heart rate to respond. Do 3 minutes of easy jogging to recover between each interval.

The Saturday run this week is between 45 and 60 minutes in length, building on your previous long runs. Don't increase the length of this run by more than 10 minutes beyond what you accomplished last week. Run a rolling to hilly course and accumulate 15 to 20 minutes in Zones 4 to 5a.

Week 4

This week builds on last week. The Tuesday workout this week is a repeat of last Tuesday's workout, with your run including 30-second accelerations. The Thursday workout this week includes three repeats of the 3-minute intervals. The intensity of the fast running is roughly 5K race pace or Zone 5b intensity with 3-minute recovery jogs between each one. Three repeats make the warm-up time quite brief, which may make the first interval feel very hard. If the second interval does not feel better, consider eliminating the intervals and just running in Zones 1 and 2. If you complete the intervals, be sure to walk after the workout to cool down.

The Saturday run this week is between 45 and 60 minutes in length, building on your previous long runs. Don't increase the length of this run by more than 10 minutes beyond what you accomplished last week. Run a rolling to hilly course and accumulate 15 to 20 minutes in Zones 4 to 5a.

Week 5

The Tuesday and Thursday workouts this week are the same as in Week 4. The long Saturday run, however, decreases in length and intensity. This is part of a short tapering and rest process to prepare you for fast running on race day. Keep your Saturday run in the 30- to 45-minute range and keep intensity in Zones 1 and 2. You can include a few short accelerations during the run, but don't get carried away.

Week 6

Race week volume is reduced so you will be fresh and fast on race day. On Tuesday, keep your run no longer than 20 minutes and do no more than three repeats of 30-second accelerations. Keep the Thursday run no longer than 20 minutes. After a warm-up, include two 60-second repeats where you build intensity from Zone 2 to race pace. Gentle, controlled speed is key. Your heart rate monitor may not reflect the intensity of your effort; use RPE instead. Take 3 minutes of easy jogging between the work intervals to recover.

On race day, try to get in a short warm-up of 10 to 15 minutes before your segment of the event. Knowing the approximate time to expect your cycling teammate in the transition area is critical. Try to run your segment of the event in a negative-split manner. (This means to run the last 1.5 miles faster than you ran the first 1.5 miles.) Note how you feel, your RPE, and your heart rate monitor reading. This information is useful for future training and racing.

Table 9.1 Fit Beginner Sprint Distance Plan for Teams—Swimmer

Week	Monday	Tuesday	Wednesday	Thursday
1	Day off	Warm up 100–300, then **swim** a 500-m time trial. Note your time and cooldown.	Day off	Warm up, then **swim** 5–6 x (50 kick, 50 swim) 10–15 sec. RI after each swim Zones 1–2
2	Day off	Warm up, then **swim** 5–6 x 100, SI equals T-Pace per 100 + 15 sec.	Day off	Warm up, then **swim** 4 x (75 kick, 75 swim) 10–15 sec. RI after each swim Zones 1–2
3	Day off	Warm up, then **swim** 3 x 200, SI equals T-Pace per 200 + 20 sec.	Day off	Warm up, then **swim** 5–7 x (25 kick, 75 swim) 10–15 sec. RI after each swim Zones 1–2
4	Day off	Warm up, then **swim** 25, 50, 75, 100, 100, 75, 50, 25. RI is 5 sec. per 25 (e.g., for 75 m RI is 15 sec.)	Day off	Warm up, then **swim** 3–4 x (100 kick, 100 swim) 15–20 sec. RI after each swim Zones 1–2
5	Day off	Warm up, then **swim** 5–6 x 100. SI equals T-Pace per 100 + 15 sec.	Day off	Warm up, then **swim** 5–7 x (75 swim, 25 kick) 10–15 sec. RI after each kick Zones 1–2
6	Day off	Warm up, then **swim** 500 with the odd-numbered 25s fast.	Day off	Warm up 10 min., then **swim** 6–8 x 25, building speed 30 sec. RI after each 25 Zones 1–2

Friday	Saturday	Sunday
Day off	Warm up, then **swim** 6–8 x 50 as fast as possible SI equals T-Pace + 1 min.	Day off
Day off	Warm up, then **swim** 6 x 50 descend. SI equals T-Pace + 1 min. Then swim 6–8 x 25 fast SI equals T-Pace per 25 + 1 min.	Day off
Day off	Warm up, then **swim** 6 x 75 (50 moderate, 25 fast) 15 sec. RI	Day off
Day off	Warm up, then **swim** 2 x 100 at T-Pace, 4 x 50 slightly faster than T-Pace, 6 x 25 all-out fast 20–30 sec. RI for all sets	Day off
Day off	Warm up, then **swim** 6 x 75 (50 fast, 10 sec. RI, 25 faster) with 1 min. RI after each 75	Day off
Day off	Race **Swim** 500	Day off

Table 9.2 Fit Beginner Sprint Distance Plan for Teams—Cyclist

Week	Monday	Tuesday	Wednesday
1	Day off	**Bike** 30 min. at mostly Zones 1–2, include 4–5 x 30 sec. accels (1 min., 30 sec. RI)	Day off
2	Day off	**Bike** 30 min. at mostly Zones 1–2, include 4–6 x 30 sec. accels (1 min., 30 sec. RI)	Day off
3	Day off	**Bike** 30 min. at mostly Zones 1–2, include 4–5 x 30 sec. right leg, 30 sec. left leg, 1 min. both legs at 90 rpm	Day off
4	Day off	**Bike** 30 min. at mostly Zones 1–2, include 5–6 x 30 sec. right leg, 30 sec. left leg, 1 min. both legs at 90 rpm	Day off
5	Day off	**Bike** 30 min. at mostly Zones 1–2, include 4 x 30 sec. right leg, 30 sec. left leg, 1 min. both legs at 90 rpm, then 4 x 30 sec. accels (1 min., 30 sec. RI)	Day off
6	Day off	**Bike** 30 min. at mostly Zones 1–2, include 4 x 30 sec. right leg, 30 sec. left leg, 1 min. both legs at 90 rpm, then 4 x 30 sec. accels (1 min., 30 sec. RI)	Day off

Thursday	Friday	Saturday	Sunday
Bike 30–45 min. total. After warm-up, do 3 x 2 min. to Zone 5b effort (2 min. RI).	Day off	Bike 1 hr.–1 hr., 15 min. on a rolling course. Accumulate 10–15 min. in Zones 4–5a, remainder in mostly Zones 1–2.	Day off
Bike 30–45 min. total. After warm-up, do 4 x 2 min. to Zone 5b effort (2 min. RI).	Day off	Bike 1 hr.–1 hr., 15 min. on a rolling course. Accumulate 15–20 min. in Zones 4–5a, remainder in mostly Zones 1–2.	Day off
Bike 45 min. total. After warm-up, do 5 x 2 min. to Zone 5b effort (2 min. RI).	Day off	Bike 1 hr.–1 hr., 15 min. After warm-up, include 3–4 x 4 min. (1 min. RI), getting into Zones 4–5a, OR if the race is hilly, ride a hilly course and get into Zones 4–5a on the climbs.	Day off
Bike 45 min. total. After warm-up, do 3 x 3 min. to Zone 5b effort (2 min. RI).	Day off	Bike 1 hr.–1 hr., 15 min. After warm-up, include 3–4 x 5 min. (2–3 min. RI), getting into Zones 4–5a, OR if the race is hilly, ride a hilly course and get into Zones 4–5a on the climbs.	Day off
Bike 45 min. total. After warm-up, do 3–4 x 3 min. to Zone 5b effort (2 min. RI).	Day off	Bike 1 hr. After warm-up, ride 20 min., getting into Zones 4–5 and holding steady, OR if the race is hilly, ride a hilly course and get into Zones 4–5a on the climbs.	Day off
Bike 30 min. at mostly Zones 1–2. Check gears and include a few accels.	Day off	Race Bike 15 miles	Day off

Table 9.3 Fit Beginner Sprint Distance Plan for Teams—Runner

Week	Monday	Tuesday	Wednesday	Thursday
1	Day off	Run 20–30 min. Include 3 x 20 sec. accels (1 min., 40 sec. RI), mostly Zone 1.	Day off	Run 20–30 min. After warm-up, include 5 min. steady Zones 4–5a.
2	Day off	Run 20–30 min. Include 3–4 x 20 sec. accels (1 min., 40 sec. RI), mostly Zone 1.	Day off	Run 20–30 min. After warm-up, include 7–10 min. steady Zones 4–5a.
3	Day off	Run 20–30 min. Include 3–4 x 30 sec. accels (1 min., 30 sec. RI), mostly Zone 1.	Day off	Run 30 min. After warm-up, include 2 x 3 min. Zone 5b (3 min. RI).
4	Day off	Run 20–30 min. Include 3–4 x 30 sec. accels (1 min., 30 sec. RI), mostly Zone 1.	Day off	Run 30 min. After warm-up, include 3 x 3 min. Zone 5b (3 min. RI).
5	Day off	Run 20–30 min. Include 3–4 x 30 sec. accels (1 min., 30 sec. RI), mostly Zone 1.	Day off	Run 30 min. After warm-up, include 3 x 3 min. Zone 5b (3 min. RI).
6	Day off	Run 20 min. Include 3 x 30 sec. accels (1 min., 30 sec. RI), mostly Zone 1.	Day off	Run 20 min. After warm-up, include 2 x 1 min., building speed to race pace (3 min. RI).

Friday	Saturday	Sunday
Day off	Run 30–45 min. on a rolling course. After warm-up, accumulate 5–10 min. in Zones 4–5a by allowing intensity to rise on hills.	Day off
Day off	Run 30–45 min. on a rolling course. After warm-up, accumulate 10–15 min. in Zones 4–5a by allowing intensity to rise on hills.	Day off
Day off	Run 45–60 min. on a rolling (or hilly) course. After warm-up, accumulate 15–20 min. in Zones 4–5a by allowing intensity to rise on hills.	Day off
Day off	Run 45–60 min. on a rolling (or hilly) course. After warm-up, accumulate 15–20 min. in Zones 4–5a by allowing intensity to rise on hills.	Day off
Day off	Run 30–45 min. in Zones 1–2	Day off
Day off	Race Run 3.1 miles	Day off

Chapter 10

Unfit Individuals on a Team
Beginner Plans for an Olympic Distance Triathlon

Nothing great was ever achieved without enthusiasm.
—Ralph Waldo Emerson

The training plans in this chapter can stand alone or be used to step up to a new distance after completing the sprint distance training plans in Chapter 8. In other words, this chapter can be used as a progression from sprint distance triathlon early in the summer to Olympic distance triathlon 6 weeks later.

Goal

Complete an Olympic distance triathlon at the end of 6 weeks of preparation. You are either the swimmer, completing approximately 1.5 kilometers (1,500 meters or 0.9 mile) of swimming; the cyclist, riding around 40 kilometers (24.8 miles); or the runner, covering around 10 kilometers (3.1 miles).

Profiles

This chapter provides a 6-week training plan for each team member. As with the unfit beginner sprint distance plan, you do not have to recruit only unfit people to your team. However, getting some friends together who have similar fitness levels can make training and racing fun.

Swimmer

As the team swimmer, you are currently capable of swimming 100 yards or meters without stopping. (For the rest of the text, you can interchange yards and meters.) You can repeat that 100-yard swim five or six times, resting 20 seconds between each repeat. The first swim workout displayed in Table 10.1 includes a 200-yard warm-up of your choice, the main set of five or six 100-yard swims, and a 100-yard cooldown. (See table at the end of this chapter.) The rest of the swim workout descriptions follow a similar format. Before beginning the plan, the first workout is easy for you to complete. Looking at Table 10.1, you can see each workout builds on the previous one.

Cyclist

You are currently riding 3 days per week. These days might include indoor riding, outdoor riding, or some combination of both. The first week of the plan shown in Table 10.2 begins with a 30- to 45-minute ride on Monday, a 45- to 60-minute ride on Thursday, and a 45- to 60-minute ride on Saturday. (See table at the end of this chapter.) A range of times is given to accommodate some individual differences. The weekday rides do not build much, however, while the long weekend rides build to between 1 hour, 30 minutes and 1 hour, 45 minutes.

Runner

The run portion of the plan in Table 10.3 displays a run/walk format. (See table at the end of this chapter.) If you have the fitness, you can run for the time indicated in the plan, rather than running and walking. Monday workouts remain at 20 minutes throughout the plan, Thursday workouts hover around 30 minutes for most of the plan, and the long weekend workouts build from 30 minutes to 50 or 60 minutes.

The Plan

Most of your workout time is spent at Zones 1 and 2 intensity. (See Chapter 3 for further information on intensity levels.) You may know specific heart rate values to define your intensity zones. If you do not have a heart rate monitor or know specific training zones at this time, you can use rating of perceived exertion (RPE) for the exercise program.

At some point during the training weeks, it is a good idea to call a team meeting to talk about logistics on race day. Can you visit the course in advance? Where is the transition area located? Does the exchange between team members involve a wristband or an ankle timing chip? These are good items to discuss prior to race day. If possible, coordinate a session to practice the handoff details, and share a pre-race celebration of fitness. Of course, the team must celebrate victory after the race as well!

All of the plans leading to race day in this chapter show workouts on Tuesday, Thursday, and Saturday. If it is more convenient for you to work out on Monday, Wednesday, and Friday, move the workouts accordingly.

Swimmer

Week 1

The plan in Table 10.1 shows your first workout on Tuesday of Week 1. The Tuesday workout assignment is to warm up for 200 yards. Use your choice of strokes on the warm-up swim. If you have the skill to do other strokes, it is fine to include them in the warm-up and cooldown. If you decide to swim using only freestyle, that is fine as well. After the warm-up, include five or six repeats of 100 yards, steady swimming. After each 100-yard repeat, rest for 20 seconds and go right into the next 100-yard swim. After completing all swims in the main set, cool down by swimming 100 yards at a very easy intensity.

On Thursday, your warm-up is 100 to 200 yards of each—swimming, kicking, and pulling (arm stroke only, no kicking, utilizing a pull buoy). After the warm-up, the main set consists of swimming eight to ten repeats of 50 yards. Break the 50-yard repeats into sets of two. The first two swims are done at the same speed. The second two 50-yard swims are at the same speed, but both are faster than the first two 50-yard swims. Keep this progression throughout the main set. The last two 50-yard swims are faster than the first two 50-yard swims. Breaking the swims into pairs of 50s that get progressively faster is noted in short-hand in the plan as 2-2-2-2-2. The Thursday workout remains the same for Weeks 1 through 5. Some swimmers will see a slight increase in speed over the course of 6 weeks so that the 50-yard repeats completed in Week 5 are, on average, slightly faster than those in Week 1.

The Saturday swim begins with a warm-up set of 100 yards of swimming, 100 yards of kicking, and 100 yards of pulling. After the warm-up set, swim a continuous 500 yards at intensity Zones 1 to 2. Learning to pace yourself during long swims is critical for race day. One helpful method is to begin the continuous swim much slower than you believe you are capable of doing. As you progress through the 500, gently increase your speed. With practice and intention, you will progress through the plan, learning the appropriate pace for race day. After the steady swim, cool down with 100 to 200 yards of very easy swimming.

Week 2

The Tuesday workout this week is similar to last week's, in that you swim 100-yard repeats; however, this week there are six or seven repeats of 100 yards. The warm-up and cooldown remain the same as in Week 1. The Thursday workout is also the same as for last week.

For the Saturday swim this week, begin with a warm-up of 200 yards of swimming and 200 yards of kicking. You can vary the strokes or keep it all freestyle, your choice. This week's main set is three repeats of 200-yard swims. After each 200 steady swim, rest for 20 seconds before beginning the next repeat. Cool down with 100 to 200 yards of very easy swimming.

Weeks 3–5

The weekly pattern remains the same as in previous weeks, with 100-yard repeats on Tuesday, 50-yard repeats on Thursday, and longer swims on Saturday. The repeats on Saturday increase to 300-yard swims in Week 3, 400-yard swims in Week 4, and 500-yard swims in Week 5.

Week 6

Race week has finally arrived. It is important to rest this week, so do not be tempted to do more swimming than shown in the plan. The Tuesday workout is only five repeats of 100 yards, with 15-second rest intervals, immediately followed by four repeats of 50 yards, with 15-second rest intervals. Each swim is at race pace. Because it is a broken swim, the pace should feel moderate on the 100s and easier on the 50s. If you are gasping for breath after each repeat, you are swimming too fast.

This week's Thursday run includes a long warm-up of 300 yards, followed by six repeats of 50 yards. The rest interval is 30 to 45 seconds between swim bouts. Swim each 50 faster than the previous one.

On race day, be sure to arrive at the venue with plenty of time to check in with your teammates and prepare for the swim. If possible, warm up for a few minutes before the starting gun. Pace your swim, as you have paced yourself in long workouts. Plan to finish the swim faster than you began.

Cyclist

Weeks 1–5

Table 10.2 displays your 6-week plan to race day. Be certain to include at least 10 minutes of warm-up time and 5 minutes of cool-down time for each workout. The Tuesday workout in Week 1 begins with a 30- to 45-minute ride at Zones 1 to 2 intensity, on a flat course and pedaling at a minimum of 90 revolutions per minute (rpm). If you do not have a cadence sensor as part of your bicycle computer, improvise by counting the number of times your right leg reaches the bottom of the pedal stroke in 15 seconds. The number should be 22 or higher. The Tuesday workout remains the same throughout the plan, with the time of the workout varying between 30 and 60 minutes.

The Thursday rides are form rides. In them, you will work on good riding form to improve your economy. In Weeks 1 and 4, your workout is isolated leg training (ILT). Most of the workout is at Zones 1 and 2 intensity. At each 10-minute mark, pedal for 30 seconds using primarily your right leg, then 30 seconds using primarily your left leg. At the top of the pedal stroke, drive your knee and toes forward. As your foot begins the downward motion, apply pressure to the pedal as if you were scraping mud off your foot on the curb of a street. As your foot moves to the back of the pedal stroke, lift and unweight your foot and prepare to drive your knee and toes forward again. If you have a "dead spot" in your pedal stroke, it will become obvious immediately during this drill. Meanwhile, the nonworking leg puts out minimal effort.

The Thursday rides in Weeks 2 and 5 include spin-up drills. After a warm-up in mostly Zones 1 to 2, include 60 seconds at 90 rpm, 60 seconds at 100 rpm, and 30 seconds at 110 rpm or faster. Recover with easy pedaling for 2 minutes, 30 seconds, then repeat the spin-up set three to five more times. Recover for 2 minutes, 30 seconds between each set.

The Thursday ride in Weeks 3 and 6 includes 30-second accelerations (accels). After a good warm-up, increase your speed over the course of 30 seconds, ending faster than you began. Recover for 1 minute, 30 seconds after each acceleration, repeating the 30-second bouts four to eight times.

The long ride is scheduled for Saturday each week. In Week 1 the ride begins at 45 to 60 minutes and builds to between 1 hour, 30 minutes and 1 hour, 45 minutes in Week 4. The Week 1 ride begins on a flat course and, as the weeks progress, you can include more hills in your rides. In Weeks 4 and 5, the course should simulate the racecourse if possible. If you consider yourself to have a good cycling base, ride at intensity Zones 1 to 3. If you are less experienced, stick to Zones 1 and 2.

Week 6

In race week, do not be tempted to train more than shown in the plan. Training volume is intentionally decreased to make sure you are rested for race day. The workouts are short and include some intensity so your legs will feel fresh for the race. On race day, you may want to warm up for about 10 minutes within the 30 minutes before you expect your team member to roll into the transition area. Plan to finish your segment of the event faster than you began. This strategy is called negative-split racing.

Runner

If you are an experienced runner, you can run for the designated workout time. Your other option is to use a combination of running and walking.

Before beginning the plan, it is important that you have appropriate running shoes. No, the tennies you use to mow the lawn each week will not work. Go to a good running gear store and ask one of the store experts for help in finding the right shoe for you.

All weekday workouts are at Zones 1 and 2 intensity. If you are an experienced runner or runner/walker, you can include Zone 3 in the longer Saturday workouts. Your goal is not to maximize Zone 3 time during these sessions.

Weeks 1–6

Tuesday workouts hold steady at 20 minutes. They alternate between weeks of 4-minute running bouts and 1-minute walking bouts, with weeks of 3-minute running bouts and 1-minute walking bouts. All of the Tuesday workouts are at intensity Zones 1 to 2.

The Thursday workouts hover between 20 and just over 30 minutes each. The run segments build in time, beginning at 5 minutes in Week 1 and building to 10 minutes in Week 4. Week 5 includes some broken running and walking at the beginning of the workout and ends with a steady run of 15 minutes.

The Saturday run in Week 1 begins with two sets of running 9 minutes and walking 1 minute. Your other option is to run for 20 minutes. If you are an experienced runner or runner/walker, you can aim for intensity in Zones 1 to 3. If you are a novice, keep to Zones 1 to 2. The number of repeats, or overall session training time, increases each Saturday to a 50- to 60-minute session in Week 5.

Week 6

If you have read the race week description of your teammates' training regimen, you know that Week 6 reduces training volume and includes rest, so you will have a better performance on race day. Don't be tempted to work out more than shown in the plan. The Tuesday and Thursday workouts are similar in structure to the workouts in Week 5. On race day, plan to run or run/walk the 6.2 miles at the same intensity you have used in training. Begin the distance at a warm-up pace and plan to run the last mile of the event faster than the first mile.

Table 10.1 Unfit Beginner Olympic Distance Plan for Teams—Swimmer

Week	Monday	Tuesday	Wednesday
1	Day off	**Warm-up:** 200 **Main set: Swim** 5–6 x 100 (20 sec. RI), Zones 1–2 **Cooldown:** 100	Day off
2	Day off	**Warm-up:** 200 **Main set: Swim** 6–7 x 100 (20 sec. RI), Zones 1–2 **Cooldown:** 100	Day off
3	Day off	**Warm-up:** 200 **Main set: Swim** 7–8 x 100 (20 sec. RI), Zones 1–2 **Cooldown:** 100	Day off
4	Day off	**Warm-up:** 200 **Main set: Swim** 8–9 x 100 (20 sec. RI), Zones 1–2 **Cooldown:** 100	Day off
5	Day off	**Warm-up:** 200 **Main set: Swim** 9–10 x 100 (20 sec. RI), Zones 1–2 **Cooldown:** 100	Day off
6	Day off	**Warm-up:** 200 **Main set: Swim** 5–6 x 100 at race pace (15 sec. RI). Go right into 4 x 50; begin at race pace and go faster on each 50 (15 sec. RI). **Cooldown:** 100	Day off

Thursday	Friday	Saturday	Sunday
Warm-up: 100–200 swim, 100–200 kick, 100–200 pull **Main set: Swim** 8–10 x 50 (30–45 sec. RI) 2-2-2-2-2 (see text) **Cooldown:** 100–200	Day off	**Warm-up:** 100 swim, 100 kick, 100 pull **Main set: Swim** 500 steady, Zones 1–2 **Cooldown:** 100–200 very easy	Day off
Warm-up: 100–200 swim, 100–200 kick, 100–200 pull **Main set: Swim** 8–10 x 50 (30–45 sec. RI) 2-2-2-2-2 (see text) **Cooldown:** 100–200	Day off	**Warm-up:** 200 swim, 200 kick **Main set: Swim** 3 x 200 (20 sec. RI), Zones 1–2 **Cooldown:** 100–200 very easy	Day off
Warm-up: 100–200 swim, 100–200 kick, 100–200 pull **Main set: Swim** 8–10 x 50 (30–45 sec. RI) 2-2-2-2-2 (see text) **Cooldown:** 100–200	Day off	**Warm-up:** 100 swim, 100 kick, 100 pull **Main set: Swim** 3 x 300 (30 sec. RI), Zones 1–2 **Cooldown:** 100–200 very easy	Day off
Warm-up: 100–200 swim, 100–200 kick, 100–200 pull **Main set: Swim** 8–10 x 50 (30–45 sec. RI) 2-2-2-2-2 (see text) **Cooldown:** 100–200	Day off	**Warm-up:** 100 swim, 100 kick, 100 pull **Main set: Swim** 4 x 400 (30 sec. RI), Zones 1–2 **Cooldown:** 100–200 very easy	Day off
Warm-up: 100–200 swim, 100–200 kick, 100–200 pull **Main set: Swim** 8–10 x 50 (30–45 sec. RI) 2-2-2-2-2 (see text) **Cooldown:** 100–200	Day off	**Warm-up:** 100 swim, 100 kick, 100 pull **Main set: Swim** 3 x 500 (30 sec. RI), Zones 1–2 **Cooldown:** 100–200 very easy	Day off
Warm-up: 300 swim, kick faster on odd-numbered lengths. **Main set: Swim** 6 x 50 (30–45 sec. RI) with each 50 faster than the previous one **Cooldown:** 100–200	Day off	Race **Swim** approximately 1,500 meters	Day off

Table 10.2 Unfit Beginner Olympic Distance Plan for Teams—Cyclist

Week	Monday	Tuesday	Wednesday	Thursday
1	Day off	Bike 30–45 min. at 90 rpm, flat course Zones 1–2	Day off	Bike 45–60 min., Zones 1–2. At each 10-min. mark, pedal 30 sec. right leg, 30 sec. left leg.
2	Day off	Bike 30–60 min. at 90 rpm, flat course Zones 1–2	Day off	Bike 45–60 min., mostly Zones 1–2. Include 3–5 x (60 sec. at 90 rpm, 60 sec. at 100 rpm, 30 sec. at 110+ rpm) (2 min., 30 sec. RIs). Spin easy to cool down.
3	Day off	Bike 30–60 min. at 90 rpm, flat course Zones 1–2	Day off	Bike 45–60 min., mostly Zones 1–2. Include 4–8 x 30-sec. accels (1 min., 30 sec. RIs).
4	Day off	Bike 30–60 min. at 90 rpm, flat course Zones 1–2	Day off	Bike 45–60 min., Zones 1–2. At each 10-min. mark, pedal 30 sec. right leg, 30 sec. left leg.
5	Day off	Bike 30–45 min. at 90 rpm, flat course Zones 1–2	Day off	Bike 45–60 min., mostly Zones 1–2. Include 3–5 x (60 sec. at 90 rpm, 60 sec. at 100 rpm, 30 sec. at 110+ rpm) (2 min., 30 sec. RIs). Spin easy to cool down.
6	Day off	Bike 30 min. at 90 rpm, flat course Zones 1–2	Day off	Bike 30 min., mostly Zones 1–2. Include 4 x 30 sec. accels (1 min., 30 sec. RIs) in the workout.

Friday	Saturday	Sunday
Day off	Bike 45–60 min., flat course Zones 1–3	Day off
Day off	Bike 1 hr.–1 hr., 15 min., rolling course Zones 1–3	Day off
Day off	Bike 1 hr., 15 min.–1 hr., 30 min., rolling course Zones 1–3	Day off
Day off	Bike 1 hr., 15 min.–1 hr., 30 min. on the racecourse or similar course profile Zones 1–3	Day off
Day off	Bike 1 hr., 15 min.–1 hr., 30 min. on the racecourse or similar course profile Zones 1–3	Day off
Day off	Race Bike 40 km (24.8 miles)	Day off

Table 10.3 Unfit Beginner Olympic Distance Plan for Teams—Runner

Week	Monday	Tuesday	Wednesday	Thursday
1	Day off	Run/Walk 20 min.: 4 x (run 4 min., walk 1 min.) Zones 1–2	Day off	Run/Walk 24 min.: 4 x (run 5 min., walk 1 min.), mostly Zones 1–2. Include 2 x 20 sec. accels within each run portion.
2	Day off	Run/Walk 20 min.: 5 x (run 3 min., walk 1 min.) Zones 1–2	Day off	Run/Walk 30 min.: 5 x (run 5 min., walk 1 min.), mostly Zones 1–2. Include 2 x 20 sec. accels within each run portion.
3	Day off	Run/Walk 20 min.: 4 x (run 4 min., walk 1 min.) Zones 1–2	Day off	Run/Walk 32 min.: 4 x (run 7 min., walk 1 min.), mostly Zones 1–2. Include 2–3 x 20 sec. accels within each run portion.
4	Day off	Run/Walk 20 min.: 5 x (run 3 min., walk 1 min.) Zones 1–2	Day off	Run/Walk 33 min.: 3 x (run 10 min., walk 1 min.), mostly Zones 1–2. Include 2–3 x 20 sec. accels within each run portion.
5	Day off	Run/Walk 20 min.: 4 x (run 4 min., walk 1 min.) Zones 1–2	Day off	Run/Walk 30 min.: 3 x (run 4 min., walk 1 min.), then run 15 min. steady, mostly Zones 1–2. Include 3–4 x 20 sec. accels within the steady run portion.
6	Day off	Run/Walk 20 min.: 5 x (run 3 min., walk 1 min.) Zones 1–2	Day off	Run/Walk 20 min.: 5 x (run 1 min., walk 1 min.), then run 10 min. steady, mostly Zones 1–2. Include 2 x 20 sec. accels within the steady run portion. **OR Run** 20 min. steady with 2–3 x 20 sec accels

Friday	Saturday	Sunday
Day off	Run/Walk 20 min.: 2 x (run 9 min., walk 1 min.), OR Run steady 20 min. Zones 1–3	Day off
Day off	Run/Walk 30 min.: 3 x (run 9 min., walk 1 min.), OR Run steady 30 min. Zones 1–3	Day off
Day off	Run/Walk 40 min.: 4 x (run 9 min., walk 1 min.), OR Run steady 40 min. Zones 1–3	Day off
Day off	Run/Walk 50 min.: 5 x (run 9 min., walk 1 min.), OR Run steady 50 min. Zones 1–3	Day off
Day off	Run/Walk 50–60 min.: 5–6 x (run 9 min., walk 1 min.), OR Run steady 50–60 min. Zones 1–3	Day off
Day off	Race Run or Run/Walk 10 km (6.2 miles)	Day off

161

Chapter 11

Fit Individuals on a Team
Beginner Plans for an Olympic Distance Triathlon

Reshape yourself through the power of your will ...
—Krishna, from *The Bhagavad Gita*

The training plans in this chapter are for fit individuals training for a team triathlon. The athletes using these plans are fit from training on their own or have gained fitness by progressing through the Chapter 10 training plans.

Goal

Complete an Olympic distance triathlon at the end of 6 weeks of preparation. You are either the swimmer, completing approximately 1.5 kilometers (1,500 meters or 0.9 mile) of swimming; the cyclist, riding around 40 kilometers (24.8 miles); or the runner, covering around 10 kilometers (3.1 miles).

Profiles

This chapter provides a 6-week training plan for each team member. If one or more of your team members are less fit than described in this chapter, they may want to use one of the training plans in Chapter 10.

Swimmer

As the team swimmer, you are currently capable of swimming 300 yards or meters without stopping. (For the rest of the text, you can interchange yards and meters.) Swimming 1,500 yards in a single workout session is easy for you. You are currently swimming 3 days per week. The first swim workout displayed in Table 11.1 includes a test set to benchmark your swimming fitness. (See table at the end of this chapter.) It is the T1b swim described in the "Swim Time Trial" section of Chapter 3. Before beginning the test set, warm up with 100 yards of swimming, 100 yards of kicking, and 100 yards of pulling. The resulting T-Pace from the test is used in many of the workouts in the plan.

Cyclist

You are currently riding 3 to 5 days per week. This can be indoor cycling, outdoor cycling, or some combination of both. At a minimum, you are cycling 2 days per week for 45 to 60 minutes and a third day is longer, 75 to 90 minutes. You are accustomed to having some intensity above Zone 2 in your workouts and the first week of training seems well within your current capability. (See Table 11.2 at the end of this chapter.) If your cycling has not had intensities in higher training zones but your endurance matches the time scheduled in the plan, you can follow the training and lower the prescribed intensity levels to meet your current capabilities.

The optional workouts shown on Mondays and Sundays are for athletes who are used to riding 4 or 5 days per week. If you find yourself pinched for time or feeling tired, the optional workouts can be eliminated.

Runner

Table 11.3 displays three running days. (See table at the end of this chapter.) Notice that the Tuesday run is 20 to 30 minutes, the Thursday run is 30 to 45 minutes, and the Saturday run is the longest workout of the week, ranging from 45 to 60 minutes. Running 3 days per week is part of your current routine and the training displayed in Week 1 is well within your capability. Some of your running is currently at intensities above Zone 2. If your running has not had intensities in higher training zones but your endurance matches the time scheduled in the plan, you can follow the training and lower the prescribed intensity levels to meet your current capabilities. You can also modify the plan to a run/walk format if you have been using that format from previous training.

The Plan

This plan assumes each athlete has built good base fitness at Zones 1 and 2 intensity, along with some time spent at higher intensities. (See Chapter 3 for further information on intensity levels.) If the first week of training in any of the plans seems too challenging, consider beginning with one of the plans in Chapter 10.

Because your team success requires orchestrating a handoff, usually in the form of a timing chip, it is a good idea to call a team meeting to talk about logistics before race day. Where is the transition area located? Does the exchange between team members involve a wristband or an ankle timing chip? If possible, coordinate a session to practice the handoff logistics and to begin the planning for the post-race celebration.

If possible, each team member should preview his or her portion of the course. Each team member should estimate a range of time for how long his or her portion of the race should take. The low-end estimate is if you have the race of your life. The high-end estimate is the time you would expect if you were having an off day. You can get these estimates from keeping pace and rating of perceived exertion (RPE) notes in a training journal. Knowing what to expect from the team on race day can help lessen anxiety. Let's look at each training plan in more detail.

Swimmer

Week 1

The training plan in Table 11.1 shows your first workout on Tuesday of Week 1. The Tuesday workout assignment is to warm up with 100 yards of swimming, 100 yards of pulling, and 100 yards of kicking. If you need more warm-up before the test set or before any of the workouts, add more distance to match your fitness.

After the warm-up, complete test T1b as described in the intensity chapter to get a benchmark pace. Your average pace for the set of three by 300s is your T-Pace. Cool down 100 to 200 yards after the test. As with the warm-up, if you need more cooldown, then adjust accordingly.

On Thursday of Week 1, the workout shows a range of yardage in the warm-up, the cooldown, and the main set. Use the yardage in this workout and all remaining workouts that best meets your current fitness needs. It is not necessary to aim for the highest number of repeats on all sets.

The main set on Thursday is broken into parts a, b, and c. For part a, you swim on a send-off time of your T-Pace plus 10 seconds. For example, if your average pace for the time trial was 1 minute, 40 seconds per 100 yards, your send-off for the first set is 1 minute, 50 seconds. The goal is to swim each 100 yards at your T-Pace. Swimming five or six repeats of 100 yards at your T-Pace, resting about 10 seconds after each swim, should be comfortable. Rest for 1 full minute after swimming five or six repeats of 100 yards.

After resting 1 minute, go right into eight to ten repeats of 50 yards. Swim these at T-Pace minus 2 or 3 seconds, or at a send-off of T-Pace plus 30 to 45 seconds. Back to the sample athlete who swam 1 minute, 40 seconds (100 seconds) per 100 yards as T-Pace: This translates to 50 seconds per 50 yards. This athlete's send-off is 80 to 95 seconds. (Push off the wall each 1 minute, 20 seconds to 1 minute, 35 seconds. Pick one send-off time and hold it throughout the set.) And he or she is swimming at a 47- to 48-second pace per 50 yards. Rest for 1 to 2 minutes after the last 50.

The main set finishes with part c, which is eight to ten repeats of 25 yards, all-out fast swimming. Pick a send-off of 30, 45, or 60 seconds and swim as fast as you can. The send-off should give you from 20 to 30 seconds of rest. After the last fast 25, cool down with an easy 200 to 400 yards.

Saturday is a long endurance-building swim. Begin with 100 to 200 yards of freestyle swimming, 100 to 200 yards swimming the stroke of your choice (butterfly, backstroke, breaststroke, or freestyle), and 100 to 200 yards of drills. Drills are not covered in detail in this book. Some example drills are single-arm swimming: eight kicks on your right side, three strokes and eight kicks on your left side, repeating the pattern; and fingertip drag with high elbows. After the warm-up, swim four repeats of 300 yards at Zones 1 to 2 intensity. This pace is slower than your T-Pace, up to 10 seconds per 100 yards slower. Try to relax and get into a comfortable rhythm. Rest 30 seconds between each 300-yard swim. Cool down 200 to 400 yards after the last 300.

Week 2

The Tuesday workout in Week 2 begins with a warm-up with your choice of swimming, kicking, pulling, and drills to total 200 to 400 yards. The main set is nine or ten repeats of 100 yards, swimming at T-Pace minus 1 to 3 seconds. The send-off is T-Pace plus 20 seconds. The sample athlete, having a T-Pace of 1 minute, 40 seconds, swims each 100 at a pace of 1 minute, 37 seconds to 1 minute, 39 seconds. After the last 100, cool down with about 200 yards of very easy swimming.

The Thursday swim is the same workout as the Thursday swim in Week 1 and repeats through Week 5. Make notes in your training journal about the paces you held and your rating of perceived exertion (RPE) during the workout.

The Saturday workout is similar to the endurance swim of Week 1. The warm-up set is the same as last week's, but the main set moves to four repeats of 400 yards. Rest 30 to 45 seconds between each swim.

Week 3

The Week 3 Tuesday swim is similar to the Tuesday swim of Week 2, with a warm-up of your choice of swimming, kicking, pulling, and drills, to total 200 to 400 yards. This week you swim eleven to twelve repeats of 100 yards, swimming at T-Pace minus 1 to 3 seconds on a send-off of T-Pace plus 20 seconds. This week, however, take a bonus rest of 1 minute when you are halfway through the set. This small amount of extra rest helps keep your pace quality high. Cool down with 200 yards of easy swimming.

As mentioned in Week 2, the Thursday swim workout is a repeat of Week 1's. The Saturday endurance swim continues to build the distance of the main set. This week is three repeats of 500 yards, resting 30 to 45 seconds between each 500. Cool down with 200 to 400 yards of easy swimming.

Week 4

The pattern continues this week, with the Tuesday main set consisting of thirteen to fourteen repeats of 100 yards, swimming at T-Pace minus 1 to 3 seconds per 100. The send-off stays at T-Pace plus 20 seconds. Halfway through the main set, rest an extra 1 minute to keep swim quality high.

The Thursday workout repeats that of previous weeks. The Saturday endurance swim has a main set of five repeats of 300 yards. Although the total distance of the main set is the same as last week's, because the distance of each swim is shorter you should swim slightly faster for the same Zones 1 to 2 perceived exertion.

Week 5

The Tuesday swim this week continues the building pattern of previous weeks. You swim fifteen to sixteen repeats of 100 yards at T-Pace minus 1 to 3 seconds per 100. The send-off stays at T-Pace plus 20 seconds, as does the bonus rest of 1 minute halfway through the set.

The Thursday swim this week is the last session repeating the Week 1 Thursday swim. Notice that you will repeat the T-Pace test on Saturday. If you are feeling tired from previous weeks of training, keep all repeats on the low end or reduce the number of repeats even more. The Saturday swim is a repeat of the T-Pace test you did on Tuesday of Week 1 (test T1b from Chapter 3). Note your times and perceived exertion in your training journal. Did you improve?

Week 6

The Tuesday swim this week begins with a warm-up set of 200 swim, 200 kick, and 200 pull. The main set is five to six repeats of 100 yards at your new T-Pace. The send-off is T-Pace plus 20 seconds. This new T-Pace is roughly your race pace. Doing only five or six repeats of 100 yards at race pace with 20 seconds of rest should feel fast enough to get your engine revved up without leaving you tired. Finish the session wanting more. Cool down with about 200 yards of swimming.

The Thursday swim is similar to that of previous weeks, but the distance is cut down by 100 per segment. The main set is six repeats of 50 yards, watch the clock, and swim each 50 faster than the previous one.

Begin slower than your T-Pace and finish slightly faster than T-Pace. Take 30 to 45 seconds between each swim. Cool down with 100 to 200 yards of easy swimming.

Saturday is race day. Arrive at the transition area with plenty of time to get checked in and to check in with your teammates. If the water is warm and the race director allows a warm-up, get in the water and swim a few hundred yards to feel good. If it is too cold or you are unable to warm up in the water for any other reason, you can warm up on dry land while waiting for your heat to swim. Move your arms gently in big circles and imitate a swimming motion to get the blood going in your upper body. If you have elastic swim cords, you can use those as well.

Swim the event in a negative-split manner, beginning the first quarter of the event at an easier pace that you think is slightly slower than T-Pace. Swim the middle half of the event at roughly T-Pace. Give the last quarter of the event all you have left. Swim fast.

Cyclist

Table 11.2 displays your 6-week plan to race day. There are three key workouts displayed on Tuesdays, Thursdays, and Saturdays. For athletes with greater fitness, optional workouts are shown on Mondays and Sundays.

Monday

The Monday workout for Weeks 1 to 5 is a 30- to 45-minute ride on a mostly flat course at a cadence of 90 revolutions per minute (rpm). If you decide to do this optional workout, take Monday of Week 6 as a day off.

Tuesday

The Tuesday workout for Weeks 1 to 5 is a 45- to 60-minute ride on a rolling course at intensity Zones 1 to 2. In Week 6, the ride profile stays the same, but the time is reduced to 30 minutes.

Thursday

The Thursday workouts include higher intensities, and you will gain the most benefit if you are rested for these sessions. Each week builds on the previous week, adding more intensity. If you begin the intervals during any week and feel tired or weak, it might be best to skip the intervals and either spin easy or go home and rest. Make that decision after beginning the second interval.

Week 1 begins the series with a good warm-up before the intervals. Each week the warm-up time is left to the athlete; however, it needs to be a minimum of 15 minutes. The intervals are four repeats of 3 minutes at Zone 3 intensity. Begin the interval timer when you begin Zone 3 RPE intensity. Know that heart rate response will lag some and you may not see Zone 3 heart rates until near the end of the first interval. Do not worry—this is normal.

Recover for 1 minute after the first interval with very easy spinning and very limited pressure on the pedals. This limited pressure is called "soft pedaling." Again, begin your interval timer as soon as you begin your Zone 3 effort. You will find your heart rate climbs into Zone 3 faster than during the first interval. Heart rate will continue this pattern in subsequent intervals, reaching Zone 3 earlier and earlier. Pay close attention to control intensity so that you are not exceeding Zone 3, for now. After four repeats, end the session with some easy spinning.

The Week 2 session is similar to Week 1's, except the work intervals are now 4 minutes long. Rest intervals remain 1 minute long. In Week 3, the work intervals remain 4 minutes long and the rest intervals remain 1 minute long; however, intensity changes to Zones 4 to 5a. Begin the intervals by aiming for low Zone 4 by the end of the first 4-minute work bout. By the end of the last interval, you can ride as fast as Zone 5a. Your goal is not to maximize Zone 5a time.

In Weeks 4 and 5, the work intervals change to 5 minutes and 6 minutes long, respectively. Rest intervals also increase to 2 minutes long. In Week 6, race week, the length of the intervals is reduced to only 90 seconds. These short intervals are designed to keep your legs feeling fast, and they are short so as not to produce too much fatigue before race day.

Saturday

The Saturday workouts are multifaceted, building overall race endurance, cycling specific strength, and race-pace speed. Week 1 begins with a ride between 1 hour, 15 minutes and 1 hour, 30 minutes in length. Ride a rolling course and include intensities in Zones 1 to 4. Be sure to include a good warm-up and read the chapter on nutrition, as you need to carry fluids and perhaps fuel on the longer rides. (See Chapter 14 for more detail on nutrition.)

After a warm-up in Week 1, accumulate around 20 minutes at Zone 4 intensity. You will need to make a reasonable estimate of this accumulated time. Do not worry if you are slightly over or under 20 minutes.

The Week 2 ride increases in length, up to 2 hours, and with 20 to 30 minutes at Zones 4 to 5a intensity.

The Week 3 ride should be on a rolling to hilly course or a course similar in profile to the racecourse. After a good warm-up, ride at all intensity levels, accumulating about 30 to 40 minutes at intensity levels of Zone 4 and above. This workout repeats in Week 4.

Week 5 ride time is reduced to allow you to begin resting for race day. Ride only 1 hour, 15 minutes to 1 hour, 30 minutes and accumulate only 20 to 30 minutes at intensity levels of Zone 4 and above.

The Saturday of Week 6 is race day. Be certain to arrive at the transition area with plenty of time to check in with your teammates, get in a warm-up, and get your bike to the designated position. The logistics of your warm-up depend on the specific instructions from the race director and on when the transition closes to further equipment additions. Your team swimmer should give you an estimated finish time so you can be prepared for the handoff. Make sure you check out all of these details before race morning.

Every racer is adrenalized and can be tempted to blast out of the transition area at breakneck speed. Control this temptation and your intensity early in the race. Try to ride the event in a negative-split manner, beginning at intensity levels of Zone 2 to Zone 3. Ride at this intensity for the first quarter of the event. In the middle half of the event, ride at intensities in Zones 4 to 5a. Bring it home with whatever you have left.

The race strategy described in the last paragraph works well for a mostly flat to rolling course. If the course is hilly, your heart rate or perceived intensity may be well above Zone 3, even early in the event.

Because you have practiced on a course similar to the racecourse, you will know how to meter your intensity so you can finish strong.

Sunday

The Sunday rides are optional. In Weeks 1 through 5, ride up to 60 minutes at mostly Zones 1 to 2 intensity. Within the workout, include six to eight repeats of 20-second accelerations. Accelerations are a gentle building of leg speed to very high cadence. By the end of the 20 seconds, you are spinning the pedals as fast as you can without bouncing your butt off the saddle. Take 1 minute, 40 seconds of recovery time between each acceleration.

To recover from the race, the Sunday ride in Week 6 is an easy spin. If the race is on Sunday instead of Saturday, make Saturday a day off or spin for 30 minutes to make sure your bike is in good working order.

Runner

The plan in Table 11.3 is for an experienced runner who currently runs 3 days per week. Your runs are routine and speed changes are very limited or nonexistent. You may run at speeds in Zone 4 for some part of every run, but most runs look very similar. This plan is designed to begin the process of giving you distinctly different gears for running and includes runs that work on economy or the ability to run faster while keeping the energy cost low.

If you are currently using a run/walk format for your program, modify the plan to meet your personal needs. If your running has included intensities limited to Zones 1 and 2, modify the plan intensities. When the plan calls for a run in Zones 1 to 5a, you will run in Zones 1 to 3.

Tuesday

Tuesday workouts begin at 20 minutes and remain between 20 and 30 minutes throughout the plan. The Tuesday run is a form run, working on cadence. Keep the workout intensity in Zones 1 and 2. Within the run, count the number of times your left (or right) foot strikes the ground in 15 seconds. The goal cadence for 15 seconds is twenty-two or more. Fast leg speed and limited time of foot-to-ground contact are two attributes of fast runners. This workout helps you begin to work on that skill.

Thursday

The Thursday workouts are between 30 and 45 minutes. This run is designed to get you to run faster without accumulating too much fatigue. The run in Week 1 begins with a warm-up of 10 minutes, followed by five to six repeats of 20-second accelerations (accels). Accelerations are the gentle building of running speed, not all-out sprints. There should be a noticeable difference between your speed at the beginning of the 20 seconds and speed at the end. Jog for 1 minute, 40 seconds between each acceleration to recover.

Week 2 has five or six repeats of 30-second accelerations with recovery intervals of 1 minute, 30 seconds. Although the acceleration time is increased, the concept remains the same—that is, to end the acceleration faster than you began. Week 3 has four or five repeats of 45-second accelerations, with 2-minute rest intervals.

Week 4 run time is between 30 and 45 minutes. If you are feeling strong and would like to increase your run time, run up to 45 minutes this week. If 30 minutes is all you can fit into your schedule, hold your run time steady. The workout this week includes four or five repeats of 60-second accelerations, with 2-minute recovery intervals. Notice that the speed change you can manage over the course of 60 seconds is different from the speed change you managed over 20 seconds. This is part of the process to get you to change gears or change your running speeds. Experimenting with different speeds begins to give you a sense of what speed is manageable for what length of time.

The Week 5 run is fun because it includes three repeats of 60-second accelerations, with 2-minute recoveries, followed by three or four repeats of 30-second accelerations with recoveries of 1 minute, 40 seconds. When you get to the 30-second accelerations, they should end at a faster pace than the 60-second accelerations.

In race week, Week 6, the workout is only 30 minutes long and includes four accelerations that are 90 seconds in length. The last 30 seconds of the acceleration is about the pace you plan to run on race day. This intensity will have your heart rate in Zones 4 to 5a. Take 3 minutes to recover between each acceleration.

Saturday

The weekend run is for building endurance and working on running at the speed you plan to run on race day. The Week 1 run is 45 minutes on a mostly flat course. Run at intensities between Zones 1 and Zone 5a. Be sure to warm up in Zones 1 to 2 before running faster speeds. Within this run, accumulate about 15 minutes at Zones 4 to 5a intensity. You will need to estimate this time. Do not worry if you are slightly under or over the accumulated time.

Week 2 is a 45- to 60-minute run on a rolling course. Accumulate about 20 minutes in Zones 4 to 5a. Week 3 is a 60-minute run on a rolling course, accumulating about 25 minutes in Zones 4 to 5a.

The run in Week 4 stays at 60 minutes, but is done in a negative-split manner. Run an out-and-back course, going out at intensity Zones 1 to 2. After 30 minutes, turn around and run back at Zones 4 to 5a effort. You should return in less time than it took you to run out. Finish with easy jogging and walking to cool down.

The Week 5 run is 45 minutes long and includes four repeats of 4 minutes, running at Zones 4 to 5a intensity and holding that intensity to the end of the interval time. Take 1 minute of easy jogging to recover between each work interval. Begin timing the work interval as soon as you begin running fast. It will take some time for your heart rate to respond. It may take you awhile to figure out what speed you can hold to keep your heart rate in the appropriate zone. Running too fast, then too easy is common for beginning runners.

Week 6 is race week. Be certain to arrive at the transition area with plenty of time to check in and check in with your teammates. Although you are the last leg of the relay team, you want to be at the event early enough to see your teammates begin their competition. Imagine how unnerving it would be for your swimmer if he or she did not see you before beginning the event.

Very experienced runners will warm up for a few minutes before the race. Others will run the event exactly like the negative-split workout in Week 4. Use all the experience from the past few weeks to run a personal best.

Table 11.1 Fit Beginner Olympic Distance Plan for Teams—Swimmer

Week	Monday	Tuesday	Wednesday
1	Day off	**Warm-up:** 100 swim, 100 kick, 100 pull **Main set: Swim** 3 x 300 (30 sec. RI), best average time **Cooldown:** 100–200	Day off
2	Day off	**Warm-up:** 200–400 choice **Main set: Swim** 9–10 x 100 at T-Pace minus 1–3 sec. Swim on a send-off time of T-Pace + 20 sec. **Cooldown:** 200	Day off
3	Day off	**Warm-up:** 200–400 choice **Main set: Swim** 11–12 x 100 at T-Pace minus 1–3 sec. Swim on a send-off time of T-Pace + 20 sec. Take 1 min. of bonus rest halfway through the set. **Cooldown:** 200	Day off
4	Day off	**Warm-up:** 200–400 choice **Main set: Swim** 13–14 x 100 at T-Pace minus 1–3 sec. Swim on a send-off time of T-Pace + 20 sec. Take 1 min. of bonus rest halfway through the set. **Cooldown:** 200	Day off
5	Day off	**Warm-up:** 200–400 choice **Main set: Swim** 15–16 x 100 at T-Pace minus 1–3 sec. Swim on a send-off time of T-Pace + 20 sec. Take 1 min. of bonus rest halfway through the set. **Cooldown:** 200	Day off
6	Day off	**Warm-up:** 100 swim, 100 kick, 100 pull **Main set: Swim** 5–6 x 100 at T-Pace minus 1–3 sec. Swim on a send-off time of T-Pace + 20 sec. **Cooldown:** 100–200	Day off

Thursday	Friday	Saturday	Sunday
Warm-up: 200–300 swim, 200–300 kick, 200–300 pull or drill **Main set: Swim** 5–6 x 100 at T-Pace. Swim on a send-off time of T-Pace + 10 sec. Rest 1 min. after the last 100. **Swim** 8–10 x 50 at T-Pace minus 2–3 sec. Swim on a send-off of T-Pace + 30–45 sec. Rest 1–2 min. after the last 50. **Swim** 8–10 x 25, all-out fast. Swim on a 30-, 45-, or 60-sec. send-off. **Cooldown:** 200–400	Day off	**Warm-up:** 100–200 freestyle, 100–200 stroke, 100–200 drill **Main set: Swim** 4 x 300 (30 sec. RI) Zones 1–2 **Cooldown:** 200–400 very EZ	Day off
Warm-up: 200–300 swim, 200–300 kick, 200–300 pull or drill **Main set: Swim** 5–6 x 100 at T-Pace. Swim on a send-off time of T-Pace + 10 sec. Rest 1 min. after the last 100. **Swim** 8–10 x 50 at T-Pace minus 2–3 sec. Swim on a send-off of T-Pace + 30–45 sec. Rest 1–2 min. after the last 50. **Swim** 8–10 x 25, all-out fast. Swim on a 30-, 45-, or 60-sec. send-off. **Cooldown:** 200–400	Day off	**Warm-up:** 100–200 freestyle, 100–200 stroke, 100–200 drill **Main set: Swim** 4 x 400 (30–45 sec. RI) Zones 1–2 **Cooldown:** 200–400 very EZ	Day off
Warm-up: 200–300 swim, 200–300 kick, 200–300 pull or drill **Main set: Swim** 5–6 x 100 at T-Pace. Swim on a send-off time of T-Pace + 10 sec. Rest 1 min. after the last 100. **Swim** 8–10 x 50 at T-Pace minus 2–3 sec. Swim on a send-off of T-Pace + 30–45 sec. Rest 1–2 min. after the last 50. **Swim** 8–10 x 25, all-out fast. Swim on a 30-, 45-, or 60-sec. send-off. **Cooldown:** 200–400	Day off	**Warm-up:** 100–200 freestyle, 100–200 stroke, 100–200 drill **Main set: Swim** 3 x 500 (30–45 sec. RI) Zones 1–2 **Cooldown:** 200–400 very EZ	Day off
Warm-up: 200–300 swim, 200–300 kick, 200–300 pull or drill **Main set: Swim** 5–6 x 100 at T-Pace. Swim on a send-off time of T-Pace + 10 sec. Rest 1 min. after the last 100. **Swim** 8–10 x 50 at T-Pace minus 2–3 sec. Swim on a send-off of T-Pace + 30–45 sec. Rest 1–2 min. after the last 50. **Swim** 8–10 x 25, all-out fast. Swim on a 30-, 45-, or 60-sec. send-off. **Cooldown:** 200–400	Day off	**Warm-up:** 100–200 freestyle, 100–200 stroke, 100–200 drill **Main set: Swim** 5 x 300 (45 sec. RI) Zones 1–2 **Cooldown:** 200–400 very EZ	Day off
Warm-up: 200–300 swim, 200–300 kick, 200–300 pull or drill **Main set: Swim** 5–6 x 100 at T-Pace. Swim on a send-off time of T-Pace + 10 sec. Rest 1 min. after the last 100. **Swim** 8–10 x 50 at T-Pace minus 2–3 sec. Swim on a send-off of T-Pace + 30–45 sec. Rest 1–2 min. after the last 50. **Swim** 8–10 x 25, all-out fast. Swim on a 30-, 45-, or 60-sec. send-off. **Cooldown:** 200–400	Day off	**Warm-up:** 100 swim, 100 kick, 100 pull **Main set: Swim** 3 x 300 (30 sec. RI), best average time **Cooldown:** 100–200	Day off
Warm-up: 100–200 swim, 100–200 kick, 100–200 pull or drill **Main set: Swim** 6–8 x 50 (30–45 sec. RI) with each 50 faster than the previous one **Cooldown:** 100–200	Day off	Race Swim 1,500	Day off

Table 11.2 Fit Beginner Olympic Distance Plan for Teams—Cyclist

Week	Monday (optional workout)	Tuesday	Wednesday	Thursday
1	Bike 30–45 min. at 90 rpm, flat course Zone 1	Bike 45–60 min. on a rolling course Zones 1–2	Day off	Bike 45–60 min. After a warm-up in mostly Zones 1–2, include 4 x 3 min., building to Zone 3 intensity and holding intensity to the end of the work interval. Take 1 min. of EZ spinning at Zone 1 between each work bout. Leave enough time to cool down at the end.
2	Bike 30–45 min. at 90 rpm, flat course Zone 1	Bike 45–60 min. on a rolling course Zones 1–2	Day off	Bike 45–60 min. After a warm-up in mostly Zones 1–2, include 4 x 4 min., building to Zone 3 intensity and holding intensity to the end of the work interval. Take 1 min. of EZ spinning at Zone 1 between each work bout. Leave enough time to cool down at the end.
3	Bike 30–45 min. at 90 rpm, flat course Zone 1	Bike 45–60 min. on a rolling course Zones 1–2	Day off	Bike 45–60 min. After a warm-up in mostly Zones 1–2, include 4 x 4 min., building to Zones 4–5a intensity and holding intensity to the end of the work interval. Take 1 min. of EZ spinning at Zone 1 between each work bout. Leave enough time to cool down at the end.
4	Bike 30–45 min. at 90 rpm, flat course Zone 1	Bike 45–60 min. on a rolling course Zones 1–2	Day off	Bike 45–60 min. After a warm-up in mostly Zones 1–2, include 4 x 5 min., building to Zones 4–5a intensity and holding intensity to the end of the work interval. Take 2 min. of EZ spinning at Zone 1 between each work bout. Leave enough time to cool down at the end.
5	Bike 30–45 min. at 90 rpm, flat course Zone 1	Bike 45–60 min. on a rolling course Zones 1–2	Day off	Bike 45–60 min. After a warm-up in mostly Zones 1–2, include 3–4 x 6 min., building to Zones 4–5a intensity and holding intensity to the end of the work interval. Take 2 min. of EZ spinning at Zone 1 between each work bout. Leave enough time to cool down at the end.
6	Day off	Bike 30 min. on a rolling course at 90 rpm Zones 1–2	Day off	Bike 30–45 min. After a warm-up in mostly Zones 1–2, include 4 x 90 sec., building to Zones 4–5a intensity and holding intensity to the end of the work interval. Take 1 min., 30 sec. of EZ spinning at Zone 1 between each work bout. Leave enough time to cool down at the end.

Friday	Saturday	Sunday (optional workout)
Day off	**Bike** 1.25–1.30 hr. on a rolling course Zones 1–4 Accumulate about 20 min. total in Zone 4	**Bike** 60 min, mostly Zones 1–2, including 6–8 x 20 sec. accels (1 min., 40 sec. RIs) within the workout
Day off	**Bike** 1.5–2 hr. on a rolling course Zones 1–5a Accumulate about 20–30 min. in Zones 4–5a	**Bike** 60 min., mostly Zones 1–2, including 6–8 x 20 sec. accels (1 min., 40 sec. RIs) within the workout
Day off	**Bike** 1.5–2 hr. on a rolling to hilly course or a course similar to the racecourse profile All zones Accumulate about 30–40 min. in Zones 4–5c	**Bike** 60 min., mostly Zones 1–2, including 6–8 x 20 sec. accels (1 min., 40 sec. RIs) within the workout
Day off	**Bike** 1.5–2 hr. on a rolling to hilly course or a course similar to the racecourse profile All zones Accumulate about 30–40 min. in Zones 4–5c	**Bike** 60 min., mostly Zones 1–2, including 6–8 x 20 sec. accels (1 min., 40 sec. RIs) within the workout
Day off	**Bike** 1.25–1.5 hr. on a rolling to hilly course or a course similar to the racecourse profile All zones Accumulate about 20–30 min. in Zones 4–5c	**Bike** 45 min., mostly Zones 1–2, including 6 x 20 sec. accels (1 min., 40 sec. RIs) within the workout
Day off	Race **Bike** 40 km (24.8 miles)	**Bike** 30–45 min. at 90 rpm, flat course Zone 1

Table 11.3 Fit Beginner Olympic Distance Plan for Teams—Runner

Week	Monday	Tuesday	Wednesday	Thursday
1	Day off	Run 20 min. Zones 1–2 Check cadence by counting right foot strikes, aim for 22+	Day off	Run 30 min. Zones 1–2 Include 5–6 x 20 sec. accels (1 min., 40 sec. RIs)
2	Day off	Run 20–30 min. Zones 1–2 Check cadence by counting right foot strikes, aim for 22+	Day off	Run 30 min. Zones 1–2 Include 5–6 x 30 sec. accels (1 min., 30 sec. RIs)
3	Day off	Run 20–30 min. Zones 1–2 Check cadence by counting right foot strikes, aim for 22+	Day off	Run 30 min. Zones 1–2 Include 4–5 x 45 sec. accels (2 min. RIs)
4	Day off	Run 20–30 min. Zones 1–2 Check cadence by counting right foot strikes, aim for 22+	Day off	Run 30–45 min. Zones 1–2 Include 4–5 x 60 sec. accels (2 min. RIs)
5	Day off	Run 20–30 min. Zones 1–2 Check cadence by counting right foot strikes, aim for 22+	Day off	Run 30–45 min. Zones 1–2 Include 3 x 60 sec. accels (2 min. RIs) followed by 3–4 x 30 sec. accels (1 min., 30 sec. RIs)
6	Day off	Run 20–30 min. Zones 1–2 Check cadence by counting right foot strikes, aim for 22+	Day off	Run 30 min. Zones 1–2 Include 4 x 90 sec. accels, building intensity into Zone 4 or 5a (1 min., 30 sec. RIs)

Friday	Saturday	Sunday
Day off	**Run** 45 min. on a mostly flat course Zones 1–5a Accumulate about 15 min. total in Zones 4–5a	Day off
Day off	**Run** 45–60 min. on a flat to rolling course Zones 1–5a Accumulate about 20 min. total in Zones 4–5a	Day off
Day off	**Run** 60 min. on a flat to rolling course Zones 1–5a Accumulate about 25 min. total in Zones 4–5a	Day off
Day off	**Run** 60 min. in a negative-split. Go out 30 min. in Zones 1–2; return, building intensity to Zones 4–5a, and hold the intensity steady. Walk to cool down. Make the course similar to the racecourse if possible.	Day off
Day off	**Run** 45 min. After a warm-up in Zones 1–2, include 4 x 4 min., building intensity to Zones 4–5a. Take 1 min. of EZ jogging between each work bout. Make the course mostly flat.	Day off
Day off	**Race** **Run** 10 km (6.2 miles)	Day off

Chapter 12

Strength Training

Perfection is not attainable, but if we chase perfection we can catch excellence.
—Vince Lombardi, legendary football coach

A strength workout is included in the designs of some of the training plans, but not all of them. The reason for this is that the first priority for getting you through a triathlon is to build your endurance for the event. As an individual competitor, your first priority is to spend time swimming, bicycling, and running. As a team member you are, of course, spending time building endurance in one of the three sports. Strength training is a valuable complement to endurance training. However, when you have limited time to prepare for an event or limited time to train within a given week, your focus needs to be on building endurance.

If you already have a strength training routine, you can continue to use your current program in place of the workouts suggested in the plan. If no strength training day is designated on the plan, you can add one if you have the time and energy for the additional workout. Try to strength train on a day that is designated as a "day off" or on a day that has a less strenuous workout. If you decide to strength train more than 1 day in a week, separate lifting days by at least 48 hours. If you find that strength training makes you sore or leaves your legs or arms feeling "dead" for endurance workouts, you may want to reduce the weight you are lifting, the number of sets, the number of repetitions, or some combination of all three.

Prior to any strength training session, warm up with 10 to 30 minutes of aerobic work. Some plans have an aerobic session of swimming, cycling, or running scheduled prior to strength training. If a specific aerobic workout is not scheduled prior to strength training, include a warm-up before hoisting weight. After each strength session, include about 10 minutes of easy cycling. Running is not suggested after a strength training session, because running on fatigued legs may put you at a higher risk for injury.

The strength training program suggested in this chapter places priority on exercises that use multiple joints and muscles in a single exercise. These exercises are intended to improve the strength of the primary muscles utilized in triathlon. As you develop a strength training and endurance routine, you can modify this program to meet your personal goals. This routine is a place to begin.

Starting a Strength Training Program

No one was born knowing how to use all the pieces of equipment in the gym, nor with perfect weightlifting form. When you're just beginning a weight-training program, ask a qualified trainer at the gym to help with setting up weight-training machines and with proper lifting form. It's a good idea to ask someone you trust to recommend a trainer, as well as to ask the trainer for his or her credentials.

When strength training, you should maintain good postural alignment whenever possible. This means when you are standing in a normal, relaxed position, the head is supported by the neck, which has a normal curvature. The neck, which is part of the spine, also has a curvature that is normal for you. For example, when doing squats, the head and neck should be in a position that allows the curvature of your neck to be in a normal position (i.e., head is not craned toward the ceiling or chin tucked in at the chest).

For any exercise, always maintain control of the weight on the concentric and the eccentric contractions. This means you should use your muscles, not momentum, to lift and lower the weight. On a concentric contraction, the working muscles are shortening to overcome the force of the weight. This motion is often called the lift phase. On an eccentric contraction, the working muscles are lengthening to resist the force of the weight. The eccentric contraction means lowering the weight using muscles to control the speed. Do not allow gravity to do all the work, and only use your muscles to stop the weight at the end of the motion.

Strength Training Phases and Exercises

The training plans in this book are between 6 and 12 weeks in length, designed for triathlon beginners or "newbies." These training plans utilize two different phases of strength training: Anatomical Adaptation and Strength Maintenance. The specifics of the phases are explained later in the chapter. When I design training plans that are longer, such as the ones found in my book *Training Plans for Multisport Athletes*, I incorporate more strength training phases and the progression is different.

The list of "Minimum Exercises" is for very busy athletes looking for efficiency. The "Recommended Additional Exercises" list is for athletes who have more time to train or who have physical weaknesses that limit race performance.

Minimum Exercises

1 Hip extension (squat, leg press, or step-up)
2 Standing bent-arm latissimus (lat) pull-down or seated cable lat pull-down
3 Supine dumbbell chest press or push-ups
4 Seated cable, low row (also called seated row)
5 Supine trunk flexion (also called abdominal curls or crunches)
6 Floor back extensions (also called "Superman")

Recommended Additional Exercises

7 Hip extension (select a different exercise than #1 above to include two hip extension exercises in your routine)
8 Knee flexion (also called hamstring curl)
9 Knee extension

10 Heel raise (also called calf raise)
11 Seated horizontal hip adduction
12 Seated horizontal hip abduction
13 Additional core body work to strengthen the trunk

Anatomical Adaptation (AA)

This is the initial phase of strength training designed for the beginning of a racing season or when an athlete is just starting a strength training program. Its purpose is to prepare tendons and muscles for greater loads in a subsequent strength training phase. Another purpose for strength training in an endurance sport program is to prepare muscles and tendons for greater sport loads, such as moving from riding a bicycle on flat terrain to rolling and hilly terrain.

Routine

Complete two or three sets of 15 to 20 repetitions (reps) of exercises 1 through 6. Exercises 7 through 13 are optional. The weight or load you lift should feel light, as if you could lift more weight. The exercises can be done in a circuit fashion, doing one set of each exercise before progressing to the second set. Or, complete one set of one exercise and rest 1 to 2 minutes before completing the second set of the same exercise. Rest 1 to 2 minutes before completing the third set. Move to the next exercise after completing all sets of one exercise.

Strength Maintenance (SM)

This phase of strength training is often used to maintain gains made in a maximal strength building phase for experienced athletes. For beginners, this phase is included to make small gains in strength without compromising endurance performance.

Routine

Keep the same exercises you used in the AA phase or, if you get pinched for time, decrease to exercises 1 through 6. On each exercise, begin with one set of 15 to 20 reps at a light weight. Increase the weight slightly and complete one or two sets of 12 to 15 reps. The load should feel moderate.

"Moderate" means challenging, but not so challenging that you must struggle to move the load. You can stop with two or three sets.

If you have the time and energy to continue, increase the load a small amount, on the hip extension exercises only, and complete one or two sets of 6 to 10 reps.

In summary:

Hip extension exercise: two to five sets

All other exercises: two or three sets

During the recovery time between exercises, stretch. Stretching exercises are outlined in Chapter 13.

Recovery Weeks

As part of this periodization plan, some weeks reduce the volume of training to allow rest and recovery. You can apply this strategy to strength training by reducing the number of strength training days that week, decreasing the time spent in each strength session by reducing the number of sets within a workout, slightly reducing the weight lifted on each exercise, or a combination of any of these three items.

Strength Exercises

The strength exercises suggested in this chapter are common exercises. Unfortunately, it is also common to perform the exercises incorrectly. For each exercise there is text that describes the start position, movement instructions, and the finish position. Additionally, a description of common errors is included. Each exercise also has a photograph displaying the start and finish positions. If your gym doesn't have equipment that looks exactly like the equipment shown in the photos, just try to find equipment that has you make a similar move. You can also ask a trainer for help. Let's begin.

Squat

Start position

- Stand with toes pointing forward, about shoulder-width apart from inside edge to inside edge.

Figure 12.1a Squat   *Figure 12.1b* Squat

Movement and finish position
- Keeping normal curvature of your back and head forward, squat until your upper thighs are about halfway to being parallel to the floor, around the same angle as the knee bend at the top of the pedal stroke when riding a bicycle. The beginning of the squat movement is similar to the movement you make to sit in a chair.
- Knees and feet remain pointed forward the entire time.
- Knees remain over the feet, not wandering in or out.
- Return to the start position.

Common errors
- Looking at the floor and bending at the waist, loosing the normal curvature of the spine at the bottom of the lift.
- Squatting too low.

- Placing the feet about 20 inches apart with toes pointing out.
- Knees rocking inward, or out, on the way up.

Stretches
- Standing quadricep stretch and standing hamstring stretch

Step-up
Start position
- Use dumbbells or a bar loaded with weight.
- Place your left foot on a sturdy platform about mid-shin high, with toes pointing straight ahead.

Movement and finish position
- Step up, using the muscles in your left leg, and touch the platform with your right foot. Pause only a moment and return to the starting position.
- Knees and feet remain pointed forward the entire time.

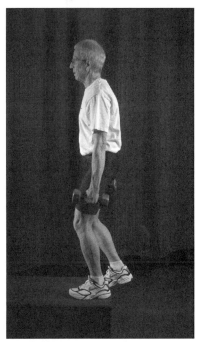

Figure 12.2a Step-up   *Figure 12.2b* Step-up

- Return to the start position.
- Complete all repetitions working the left leg, then repeat with the right leg.

Common errors
- Looking at the floor and bending at the waist.
- Allowing the toes to point out.
- Allowing the knees to sway in or out.
- Toeing off the bottom leg. In the movement description above, that would be pushing off the right leg to make the step, instead of using the muscles in the left leg to make the motion.

Stretches
- Standing quadricep stretch and standing hamstring stretch

Leg Press
Start position
- If the seat is adjustable, make the angle of the seat so that there is about an arm's length between your torso and your knees.
- Place your feet flat on the platform about 8 inches apart with toes pointing forward, aligned with your knees.

Movement and finish position
- Press the platform away from you, until your legs are straight and knees are almost locked.
- Lower the platform until your upper and lower legs form an 80- to 90-degree angle.
- Knees and feet remain pointed forward and about shoulder-width apart the entire time.
- Keep your knees aligned with your hips and toes during the entire motion up and down.
- Return to the start position.

Common errors
- Placing feet too high on the platform, such that the ankles are in front of the knee joints.

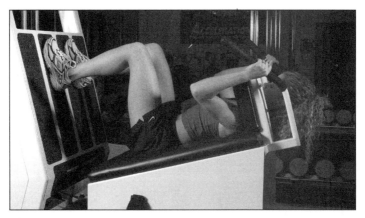

Figure 12.3a Leg Press

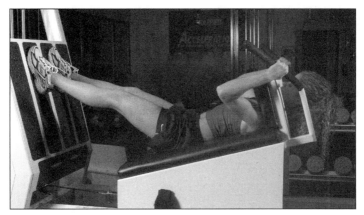

Figure 12.3b Leg Press

- Placing feet too low so that heels hang off the platform.
- Raising heels off the platform during the lift phase.
- Lowering the platform so that your knees touch your chest. This generally relaxes some of the muscles that should be working, lifts your butt off the seat pad, rocks your pelvis forward, and eliminates the normal curvature of the spine.
- Not controlling the weight in both directions.

Stretches
- Standing quadricep stretch and standing hamstring stretch

Figure 12.4a Standing Bent-Arm
Lat Pull-down

Figure 12.4b Standing Bent-Arm
Lat Pull-down

Standing Bent-Arm Lat Pull-down
Start position
- Grasp the bar with arms extended, arms bent at the same angle as during freestyle swimming.
- Step back enough to lift the weights off the stack while arms are extended in the start position.
- Knees are bent and feet are about shoulder-width apart.

Movement and finish position
- Pull the bar toward your thighs, by first depressing the shoulders away from your ears, then retracting the shoulder blades—pulling them together.
- Follow by pulling with the arms.
- Pause for a moment.
- Return the weight to the start position by moving the arms, then the shoulders.

Common errors

- Jerking the weight to begin and using a lot of torso movement to get the weight started (using your body weight instead of back and arm muscles to move the weight).
- Relaxing the muscles when returning the weight to the start position and allowing the weight to jerk the arms, instead of using back and arm muscles to control the weight on the return to the start.

Stretches

- Standing upper torso stretch

Seated Cable Lat Pull-down

Start position

- Grasp the bar with arms fully extended and hands about shoulder width apart, using an overhand grip.
- Sit down on the bench, feet flat on the ground, and knees bent at about a 90-degree angle.
- Adjust the thigh pads so they help keep you seated.

Figure 12.5a Seated Cable Lat Pull-down   *Figure 12.5b* Seated Cable Lat Pull-down

Movement and finish position
- Leaning back slightly, pull the bar toward the upper chest, by first depressing the shoulders away from your ears, followed by pulling with the arms.
- Pull down and in until the bar just touches or is very close to the breastbone.
- Pause for a moment.
- Return the weight, moving the arms, then the shoulders.

Common errors
- Jerking the weight and using a lot of torso movement.
- Leaning back to get the weight started (using your body weight instead of your muscles to move the weight).

Stretches
- Standing upper torso stretch

Supine Dumbbell Chest Press
Start position
- Lie on your back on a bench with your back in a neutral position, one that allows normal curvature.
- Feet touch the floor or are on the bench, whichever position is most comfortable.
- Weights are held in the hands, aligned with the elbows and shoulder joints. (A barbell can be used when going to heavier weight.)

Movement and finish position
- Retract the shoulders—squeeze your shoulder blades together.
- Lower the weight, by leading with your elbows, until your elbows align with your shoulder joints.
- Your forearm remains perpendicular to the floor throughout the movement.
- Pause for a moment and return to the start position by keeping your hands directly above your elbows throughout the movement.

Common errors
- Allowing the dumbbells to drift toward the centerline of the body or away from the body on the upward movement.
- Arching your back when lifting heavier weights.
- Not retracting the shoulders.

Stretches
- Standing upper torso stretch

Figure 12.6a Supine Dumbbell Chest Press

Figure 12.6b Supine Dumbbell Chest Press

Push-up
Start position
- Begin with hands slightly wider than the shoulders, fingers pointing forward or slightly in.
- The floor contact points are the hands and either the knees or toes.

Movement and finish position
- Keeping the body rigid, abdominal muscles tight, push your chest away from the floor until your elbows are extended and nearly locked.
- Lower the body back toward the floor, in a controlled manner, until the angle between the upper and lower arms is between 90 and 100 degrees.
- Pause for a moment before pushing back up again.
- Keep the head aligned with the body, as if you were in a standing position.
- Repeat the action until all repetitions are complete.

Common errors
- Relaxing all muscles on the downward motion.
- Allowing the body to sag in the middle, arching the back.

Stretches
- Standing upper torso stretch

Figure 12.7a Push-up

Figure 12.7b Push-up

Seated Cable, Low Row
Start position
- Use a handle that puts your hands in a position similar to the one you use when holding the hoods of your bicycle handlebars. At many gyms there are many handles to choose from. Use the widest one, or use one of the short bars available at most gyms and put your hands the same distance apart as if you were holding the handlebar top.
- Seated, with your torso and thighs, or upper legs, forming nearly a 90-degree angle, place your feet flat on the footplates.
- Head and neck are upright, eyes looking forward.
- Elbows are nearly straight when handles are held at arm's length and there is tension in the cable.
- Shoulder blades are relaxed and separated (abducted).

Movement and finish position
- Initiate the pull by retracting the shoulder blades together, then pulling the bar toward the chest, leading with your elbows.
- After a brief pause at the chest, return the handle to the start position by moving first at the elbows, then the shoulders.
- After the elbows are nearly straight, allow the shoulder blades to separate slightly, returning to the start position.
- The back should remain still throughout the entire exercise, only

flexing to return the bar to the floor when the exercise is complete.
• Abdominal muscles remain contracted to stabilize the torso.

Common errors
• Flexing or bending at the waist and using the back to initiate the movement.
• Not abducting the shoulder blades first in order to train the muscles of the upper back.

Stretches
• Standing upper torso stretch

Figure 12.8a Seated Cable, Low Row

Figure 12.8b Seated Cable, Low Row

Abdominal Curl

Start position

- Lying on your back, bend your knees so your feet rest comfortably on the floor.
- Hands are behind the head for support (do *not* pull on the head) or crossed on the chest.
- Feet are flat on the floor.

Movement and finish position

- Contract your abdominal muscles, bringing your bottom ribs toward your hip bones.

Figure 12.9a Abdominal Curl

Figure 12.9b Abdominal Curl

- Your shoulders, neck, and head follow.
- You are as far as you can go when your feet begin to rise off the floor.
- Pause for a moment, keeping your feet on the floor.
- Lower yourself slowly until you are just before the point of losing the contraction on your abdominal muscles. In other words, don't relax on the floor before the next repetition.

Common errors
- Pulling on your head with your hands.
- Using a rocking motion and momentum, instead of controlling the movement.

Stretches
- While lying on the floor on your back, stretch your hands and feet in opposite directions along the floor.

Floor Back Extension (Single Arm and Single Leg)
Start position
- Lying facedown on the floor, place your arms forward.

Movement and finish position
- Using your back muscles, raise one arm and the opposite leg off the ground, keeping your pelvic bones on the floor. (Note: A more advanced move is to raise both arms and both legs off the floor.)
- Your neck remains aligned with your spine, maintaining its normal curvature.
- Pause for a moment.
- Keeping your back muscles contracted, lower arm and leg back to the starting position.
- Switch to the other arm and the other leg.

Common errors
- Attempting to use your head and momentum to get your arm and leg off of the floor.
- Totally relaxing the back muscles when returning to the start position.
- Hyperextending the neck, pushing the chin toward the ceiling.

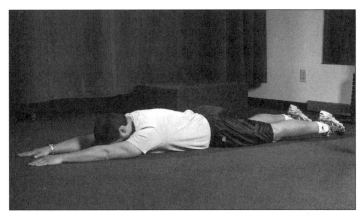

Figure 12.10a Floor Back Extension

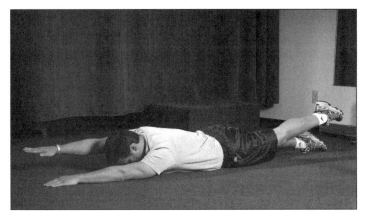

Figure 12.10b Floor Back Extension

Stretches
- Seated hip, back and gluteus stretch

Knee Flexion

Start position
- Begin with the support pad a few inches above your heels.
- Align the center of your knee joint with the pivot point on the equipment.
- Relax your foot; don't try to flex it.

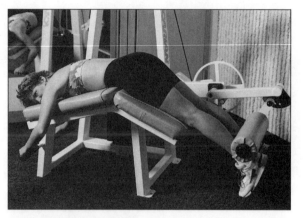

Figure 12.11a Knee Flexion

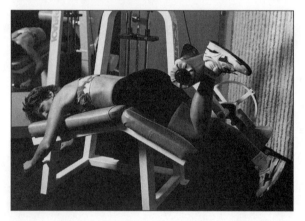

Figure 12.11b Knee Flexion

Movement and finish position
- Curl one leg up as far as possible.
- Pause for a moment.
- Return the rotating arm to the start position, keeping the hamstring muscles contracted.
- Complete all repetitions in a set with one leg before switching to the other leg.

Common errors
- Stopping short by not curling the leg as far as possible.
- Relaxing the hamstring muscles when lowering the weight.

- Arching the back to complete the lift.
- Using momentum to complete the lift.

Stretches
- Standing hamstring stretch

Knee Extension
Start position
- Begin with both legs fully extended, lifting a weight you can lift with a single leg.
- The seat should be adjusted so you have back support and the center of your knee joint aligns with the pivotal joint on the exercise equipment.
- Keep knees and hips aligned throughout the exercise.

Movement and finish position
- Use one leg to lower the weight about 8 inches or just before the point where your quadriceps muscles lose contraction. (Do not go all the way down.)
- Return to the starting position and pause for a moment.
- Complete all repetitions in the set with one leg before switching to the other leg.

Figure 12.12a Knee Extension

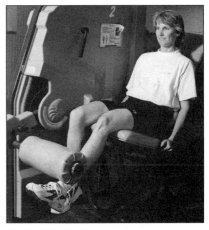

Figure 12.12b Knee Extension

Common errors

- Lowering the weight past the point where the quadriceps muscles contracted. (You can put your hand on your quadriceps and feel when they are contracted and tight and when they are relaxed.)
- Using momentum to swing the weight up and down, instead of using a controlled motion.
- Arching the back in the lift phase.
- Allowing your butt to lift off the seat pad.
- Allowing your knees to rotate in or out.

Stretches

- Standing quadricep stretch

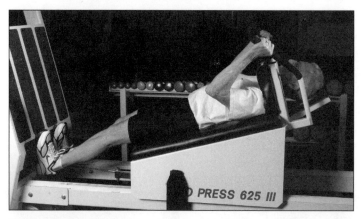

Figure 12.13a Heel Raise

Figure 12.13b Heel Raise

Heel Raise
Start position
- Use a leg press machine, standing calf-raise machine, or a riser block.
- If using a leg press or a standing calf-raise machine, you can work both legs at once or one at a time.
- Using a riser block, you can either use your body weight or hold a dumbbell.
- Doing single- or double-leg heel raises, point the toe of the working leg(s) forward.
- The ball of your foot is on the platform and the heel is as low as possible, allowing you to maintain an eccentric contraction in the calf muscle. (Calf muscle is not totally relaxed.)
- Knee is straight but not locked out.

Movement and finish position
- From the heel-down position, contract your calf (push up onto your tip-toes) until you are on the ball of your foot, as high as you can go.
- Pause for a moment at the top position.
- In a controlled manner, return to the start position.
- If you are doing single-leg exercises, complete all repetitions in a set with one leg, then switch legs.

Common errors
- Not going as high as possible.
- Going too low and losing tension on the calf muscle.
- Relaxing the muscles on the down motion.
- Not doing the exercise in a controlled manner.

Stretches
- Standing lower leg stretch

Standing Machine Hip Adduction
Start position
- Stand comfortably with spine in neutral alignment. (Do not arch your back or lean forward.)

Figure 12.14a Standing Machine Hip Adduction   *Figure 12.14b* Standing Machine Hip Adduction

- The pad on the machine is just above your knee on the inside.
- The angle of the padded arm should cause a very slight, but not excessive, stretch on the adductors (inner thigh).

Movement and finish position
- Move the leg toward the midline of the body.
- Move across the midline of the body without twisting your torso.
- Pause for a moment and return to the start position by controlling the speed of the weight.

Common errors
- Arching the back.
- Swinging and twisting the torso, not keeping hips facing the machine.
- Beginning with an excessive stretch on the adductors.

Figure 12.15a Standing Machine Hip Abduction

Figure 12.15b Standing Machine Hip Abduction

- Moving the weight with an explosive start.
- Relaxing muscles on the return to start and allowing the weight to slam down.

Stretches
- Seated adductor stretch

Standing Machine Hip Abduction
Start position
- Stand comfortably with spine in neutral alignment. (Do not arch your back or lean forward.)
- The pad on the machine should be just above your knee on the outside.
- The angle of the padded arm should cause a very slight, but not excessive, stretch on the abductors (outer thigh).

Movement and finish position
- Keeping your trunk stable, move the working leg away from the midline of the body.
- Pause for a moment and return to the start position by controlling the speed of the weight.

Common errors
- Arching the back.
- Swinging and twisting the torso, not keeping hips facing the machine.
- Moving the weight with an explosive start.
- Relaxing muscles on the return to start position and allowing the weight to slam down.

Stretches
- Seated hip and gluteus stretch

References

Bernhardt, Gale. *The Female Cyclist: Gearing up a Level.* Boulder, CO: VeloPress, 1999.

Brooks, Douglas, M.S. *Effective Strength Training: Analysis and Technique for Upper Body, Lower Body, and Trunk Exercises.* Champaign, IL: Human Kinetics, 2001.

Chapter 13

Stretching

Men are born soft and supple; dead, they are stiff and hard. Plants are born tender and pliant; dead, they are brittle and dry. Thus whoever is stiff and inflexible is a disciple of death. Whoever is soft and yielding is a disciple of life. The hard and stiff will be broken. The soft and supple will prevail.

—Lao-tzu, sixth century B.C.,
Chinese philosopher, founder of Taoism

There are two basic types of flexibility: static flexibility and dynamic flexibility. Static flexibility is the range of motion relative to a joint, with little emphasis on speed of movement. An example is hamstring, back, and upper back flexibility for people trying to ride in a time trial position or for those enduring a long ride. Dynamic flexibility is resistance to motion at the joint and involves speed during physical performance. An example of dynamic flexibility is a short sprint run to pass a fellow competitor at the finish line. A good triathlete must have both types of flexibility.

Flexibility has been shown to improve neuromuscular coordination, physical efficiency, balance and muscular awareness and performance. It increases blood supply and nutrients to joint structure and improves strength.

A study of swimmers, football players, and runners considered the benefit of contract–relax flexibility training for the knee extensors and flexors. Contract–relax flexibility training involves a passive stretch of a muscle after an isometric contraction. The athletes did flexibility training for 8 weeks, 3 days per week. The researchers found flexibility training increased the range of motion of the knee joint by about 6 percent. The scientists also found the stretching improved knee joint torque. Eccentric knee extension torque increased between 19 and 25 percent, depending on the particular velocity of measurement. Eccentric knee flexion torque increased by 16 and 18 percent, again depending on the velocity of measurement. Concentric knee flexion torque increased between 8 and 10 percent, while knee flexion isometric torque increased by 11 percent.

In summary, the contract–relax flexibility training increased the strength of the knee flexors and extensors (hamstrings and quadriceps, respectively, to name some of the major muscles) during eccentric actions. The training also increased the strength of the knee flexors during concentric actions.

How to Stretch

Good times to stretch are after your cooldown, following an aerobic session, and during rest periods between strength training sets. There are many methods for stretching. The one recommended in this book is called "proprioceptive neuromuscular facilitation" (PNF). There are also many variations on this technique. One easy-to-follow version is:

1 Static stretch and hold the muscle for about 8 seconds—remember to breathe.
2 Contract or flex the same muscle for about 8 seconds. (Leave out the contraction step when stretching during the rest interval of strength training and just hold static stretches for about 15 seconds.)
3 Stretch and hold the stretch, again, for about 8 seconds—breathe.
4 Continue alternating muscle contractions and stretches until you have completed four to eight static stretches. End with a stretch and not a contraction.

Each time you repeat the stretch, you should find you can stretch farther, or increase your range of motion.

Stretches for Cycling and Weight Room

Some of the exercises stretch multiple muscles, so they can save time for the hurried athlete. It is best if they are done in the order they are listed. Some of these stretches may or may not work for you. If you want further ideas for stretching exercises, a couple of good resources are the books *Sport Stretch* by Michael J. Alter and *Stretching* by Bob Anderson.

Figure 13.1 Standing Quadriceps Stretch

Standing Quadriceps Stretch

- While balancing against something with your left hand, grasp your right foot behind your butt.
- Static stretch by gently pulling your foot up and away from your butt.
- Stand erect and keep your hip, knee, and ankle in alignment.
- Contract by pushing against your hand with your foot. Begin with a gentle force.
- Repeat with the left leg.

Common errors
- Pulling the foot against the butt and compressing the knee joint.
- Bending over at the waist.

Figure 13.2 Standing Hamstring Stretch

Standing Hamstring Stretch
- Bend over at the waist, balancing yourself against something stable.
- Place the leg to be stretched forward and place your other leg behind the front leg about 12 inches, toes pointing forward.
- With your weight mostly on the front leg, press your chest toward the front kneecap and relax your back muscles.
- You should feel the stretch in the hamstring muscles of the front leg.
- Contract the front leg by trying to pull it backward against the floor—there is no movement.
- Repeat with the other leg.

Common errors
- Allowing the toes to point out.
- Not relaxing the back muscles.

Figure 13.3 Standing Upper Torso Stretch

Standing Upper Torso Stretch
Stretches the latissimus dorsi, trapezius, pectoralis, and triceps muscles.
- Hold on to something stable for support, hands placed slightly wider than shoulder-width, feet about shoulder-width apart, and knees slightly bent.
- Allow your head to relax between your arms.
- For the contraction phase, push against the support with your arms, contracting the muscles in your upper back.

Common errors
- Not relaxing all the muscles in the arms, chest, and upper back.

Seated Back, Hip, and Gluteus Stretch
Stretches the gluteus, tensor fasciae latae, and latissimus muscles, as well as the iliotibial tract.
- Sit on the ground with one leg extended in front of you and the opposite hand behind your back for support.
- Cross one foot (the left foot is used in Figure 13.4) over the opposite (right) leg and slide your (left) heel toward your butt.
- Place your right elbow on the outside of your left knee.

- Look over your left shoulder while turning your torso. Gently pushing on your knee with your right elbow increases the stretch.
- Hold the stretch for 15 to 30 seconds.
- Contract by pushing your knee against your elbow, resisting the force with your elbow.
- Repeat with the other leg and arm.

Common errors
- Keeping shoulders, back, and butt muscles tense—take a deep breath and relax.

Figure 13.4 Seated Back, Hip, and Gluteus Stretch

Seated Adductor Stretch
Stretches the adductor magnus, adductor brevis, adductor longus, pectineus, and gracilis.
- Sit on the ground with your spine in a natural position, not leaning forward or backward. (You can also put your back against a wall.)
- Grasp your ankles and pull them toward you, enough to feel a light stretch.
- Place elbows on your inner legs and gently push your legs toward the floor.
- Contract by pushing your legs upward against your elbows, elbows resisting the push.

Common errors
- Rounding your back.
- Pushing too hard on the inner legs.

Figure 13.5a Seated Adductor Stretch   *Figure 13.5b* Seated Adductor Stretch

Standing Lower Leg Stretch
Stretches the gastrocnemius, soleus, and Achilles tendon.
- Lean against an immovable support object, with the leg to be stretched straight behind you and your other leg forward.
- Toes point forward.
- Press the heel of the back leg into the ground and move your hips forward, keeping your back knee straight. The farther forward you press your hips, the more stretch you should feel in the back leg's lower muscles.

Figure 13.6a Standing Lower Leg
Stretch

Figure 13.6b Standing Lower Leg
Stretch

- Then, slightly bend the back knee to stretch different calf muscles.
- Contract the calf muscles by pushing against the support object as if you were pushing it away using your back leg.

Common errors
- Pointing the toes in or out.
- Not putting most of your weight on the back leg.

References

Alter, Michael J. *Sport Stretch*. Champaign, IL: Human Kinetics, 1998.

Anderson, B. *Stretching*. Bolinas, CA: Shelter Publications, 1980.

Bernhardt, Gale. *The Female Cyclist: Gearing up a Level*. Boulder, CO: VeloPress, 1999.

Chapter 14

Nutrition

If we could give every individual the right amount of nourishment and exercise,
not too little and not too much, we would have found the safest way to health.
—Hippocrates, Greek physician born in 460 B.C.,
known as the Father of Medicine

A January 2004 search of books on the subject of "diet" on the Amazon
Web site yields 74,620 results. No doubt, diet and nutrition have been a
hot topic for years and remain so. The intent of this chapter is not to discuss nutrition topics in great detail, but rather to give general information and guidelines that are applicable to training and racing in
endurance sports. If you are interested in reading in greater detail about
diet and nutrition, a list of resources to get you started is included at the
end of this chapter.

Few people would argue that eating a wide variety of nutrient-dense,
minimally processed foods is good for overall health. The arguments
attend the varied (and often conflicting) recommendations of exactly
what quantities to eat of which foods. I have yet to find scientific proof
that one single diet plan is the solution for *all* individuals, producing optimal health and wellness. Part of the reason that one size does not fit all is

that each of us has been dealt a unique deck of genetic cards. Due to heredity, when two people precisely follow the same diet, one person might achieve optimal health, while the second might not. In addition to heredity cards, each of us has a different lifestyle. The nutrition needs of someone who stays fit by walking 20 minutes three times per week are different from those of an endurance athlete. The detailed nutrition needs of an age-group athlete training for and racing a 1-hour sprint triathlon are different from the needs of an age-group ironman-distance racer training for an event that will take some 13 to 17 hours to complete.

Because the focus of this book is sprint and Olympic distance racing, not half- and full-ironman distances, you can utilize a couple of the commonly published guidelines for training and racing:

For all workouts and races longer than 1 hour, consume 4 to 8 ounces of fluid every 15 to 20 minutes. One bike bottle of fluid typically holds between 16 ounces for the small size and 24 ounces for the larger bottles.

For all workouts and races longer than 1 hour, consume approximately 150 to 250 calories per hour. The calories you consume can be in the form of a sports drink, or the calories can come from gels, sports bars, or homemade fuels such as jelly sandwiches.

These numbers need to be adjusted individually for large and small people. Small people can aim for the low end of the range and larger people may do better if they have more than 250 calories. To find the values that serve you best, some experimentation and testing during training are required. Always test your race day plan in training sessions. Experimenting with new foods on race day can lead to unwelcome surprises.

It is important to know that the guidelines discussed in the previous paragraphs work well for training and racing for lengths of time between 1 and 3 hours. As events get longer, such as for ironman-distance training and racing, the guidelines need upward adjustment—more calories need to be consumed. Some ironman-distance racers consume in excess of 500 calories per hour during a race. Should you decide to race longer distances in the future, understand that your fueling and hydrating plan will need adjustment.

As you progress in your training and racing for sprint and Olympic distance events, calorie consumption and energy balance may become more important. Some athletes want to lose a few pounds, some want to maintain weight, while others want to gain weight and strength. To simplify the cause-and-effect of your eating, if you consume calories equal to your caloric expenditure, your body weight will remain stable. If your calorie consumption is lower than your caloric energy expenditure, you will lose weight. If you eat more calories than your body needs, the additional calories are stored as fat. Some stored fat is essential for good health, and endurance athletes utilize stored fat to provide the body with energy in training and races. To begin looking at energy balance, a few reference formulas are handy:

1 To sustain your daily lifestyle (without taking workouts into consideration), you need to consume approximately 30 calories per kilogram of body weight. To find your weight in kilograms, take weight in pounds and divide by 2.2. For example, if weight is 140 pounds, weight in kilograms is $140 \div 2.2 = 63.6$, or approximately 64 kilograms. To calculate your total daily caloric needs, the formula is 64 kilograms x 30 calories = 1,920 calories.
Formula 1 is a baseline value, and this value may need modification depending on your job or daily lifestyle.
2 Add more calories if you lead a highly active lifestyle or subtract calories if your daily tasks are sedentary—100 to 300 calories may be appropriate.

Formulas 1 and 2 take into consideration your base metabolism and daily, non-endurance activities—your job or whatever you do with your non-athletic daytime hours. The following formulas estimate your energy needs for triathlon-related workouts:

Swim: Add about 0.13 to 0.16 calorie per minute, per kilogram of body weight, for swimming. (For example, 0.16 calorie/minute-kilogram x 60 minutes x 64 kilograms equals 614 calories needed for an hour of fast swimming.)

Bike: Add about 0.15 to 0.17 calorie per minute, per kilogram of body weight, for cycling. (For example, 0.17 calorie/minute-kilogram x 60 minutes x 64 kilograms equals 653 calories needed for an hour of fast cycling.)

Run: Add about 0.14 to 0.29 calorie per minute (roughly the range from an 11-minute pace per mile to a 5-minute, 30-second pace per mile), per kilogram of body weight, for running. (For example, 0.2 calorie/minute-kilogram x 60 minutes x 64 kilograms equals 768 calories needed for an hour of fast running.)

Weight training: Add about 0.1 calorie per minute, per kilogram of body weight, for strength training. (For example, 0.1 calorie/minute-kilogram x 60 minutes x 64 kilograms equals 384 calories needed for an hour of strength training.) Assuming your sample 64-kilogram athlete has an active job requiring an additional 300 calories per day, his or her baseline intake to maintain body weight is approximately 2,220 calories per day. Adding 30 minutes of swimming to the day would require him or her to consume an additional 250 calories that day. (0.13 calorie/minute-kilogram x 30 minutes x 64 kilograms equals 250 calories.)

If you experience a fading feeling during training or your body weight is not helping you perform as you would like to, you need to evaluate your food and drink intake. Write down everything you eat and drink for a few days and in what quantities. By knowing approximate calorie intake and calorie expenditure, you can begin to determine your energy balance. A few words of caution: If you are looking to drop body weight, running a daily calorie deficit of 200 to 300 calories will result in a gradual weight loss. Gradual weight loss accomplished by healthy long-term eating and exercise habits yields a lower body weight that you can maintain. Big daily calorie reductions usually lead to poor exercise performance, foul moods, poor sleep, and yo-yo body weight values. Think of "diet" as a long-term way of eating. There is no quick fix. Short-term, drastic attempts at weight loss usually lead to short-term results.

The fuels you use in training are, of course, included in your daily caloric count. Earlier in the chapter I mentioned that during training and races longer than an hour, you need to consume 150 to 250 calories per hour. This calorie estimate comes from a well-published and generally accepted guideline that calls for consumption of 30 to 60 grams of carbohydrate per hour of intense or long exercise—at a minimum. There are 4 calories per gram of carbohydrate, 4 calories per gram of protein, and 9 calories per gram of fat. With 4 calories per gram of carbohydrate, the same guideline recommends consuming 120 to 240 carbohydrate calories per hour. For this chapter, I have simply rounded the numbers up to the nearest multiple of 50.

The guideline mentioned in the last paragraph and the other recommendations listed in the chapter work well for training and during the race. But what about race day? More specifically, what should happen on race morning?

Often, athletes discover they have so many butterflies in their stomach on race morning that they feel unable to eat. Topping off your fuel tank on race morning is important, because you have been sleeping for several hours without food or fluids. You need to give your pre-race meal some thought and experiment with different foods during training to see what works well for you. Even though you practice pre-race fueling during training, there is a chance that on race morning you won't feel like eating anything. Know this during your training experiments and look for foods that you can eat even when your stomach is queasy.

To help you begin your personal experiment, here's a guideline for pre-race fueling:

Race morning: For race morning breakfast, consume 1 to 4 grams of carbohydrates per kilogram of body weight 1 to 4 hours before the start of the race. If you eat 4 hours prior to race start, eat more than if you eat only 1 hour before

race start. Some protein and fat in the pre-race meal are
fine, but keep it minimal. The exact amount of fat and
protein that can be consumed before race start seems
to vary among individuals. Using our 64-kilogram athlete as an example, if he or she eats 4 hours prior to race
start, pre-race fueling is approximately 4 grams of carbohydrates x 64 kilograms of body weight = 256 grams of
carbohydrates. At 4 calories per gram of carbohydrate,
this translates to approximately 1,024 calories. If our
athlete is eating only 1 hour before the race, 1 gram of
carbohydrate per kilogram may work better, resulting in
a pre-race meal of 64 grams of carbohydrates or 64
grams of carbohydrates x 4 calories = 256 calories.

I hope this chapter has armed you with enough information to help
you determine your fueling and hydration needs for training and racing
in triathlon or other endurance events. You now have enough basic information to begin an evaluation of your own overall energy needs. The
formulas are handy guidelines, but you need to experiment some and
collect your own data to find the fueling combinations that work best for
you. Just as in physical training, achieving proper nutrition requires
strategy and planning. As you continue your adventures in triathlon,
make sure you have enough high-quality fuel and fluids to propel you to
great performances.

Further Reading

Bernhardt, Gale, *Training Plans for Multisport Athletes.* Boulder, CO:
VeloPress, 2000.

Burke, Louise, Ph.D. *The Complete Guide to Food for Sports Performance: Peak
Nutrition for Your Sport.* 2nd ed. St. Leonards, Australia: Allen & Unwin, 1996.

Coleman, Ellen, R.D., M.A., M.P.H. *Eating for Endurance.* Boulder, CO: Bull
Publishing Company, 1997.

Cordain, Loren, Ph.D. *The Paleo Diet: Lose Weight and Get Healthy by Eating the
Food You Were Designed to Eat.* John Wiley & Sons, 2002.

Ryan, Monique. *Complete Guide to Sports Nutrition*. Boulder, CO: VeloPress, 1999.

Ryan, Monique. *Sports Nutrition for Endurance Athletes*. Boulder, CO: VeloPress, 2002.

Epilogue

In late 2003, as I was writing this book, I was interviewed by *USA Today* columnist Vicki Michaelis. She asked about the first time triathlon was included in the 2000 Olympic Games in Sydney, Australia. Her questions and our discussion spanned a wide range of subjects related to triathlon. That telephone interview sent me on a subsequent search for information buried in old magazines in my office closet, all neatly categorized by year. The information I found changed Chapter 1 of this book.

In addition to being an information mining expedition, the search turned into a dream-weaver journey, hours long, as I sat on my office floor reading triathlon history. This history was lived and documented by many of the legends in the sport of triathlon still living. I've had the good fortune to meet many of those people. Man, I'm a lucky dog!

During my daydream voyage, images and words from these old magazines triggered memories of my own experiences in the sport. I recognized once more how much fun and health, and how many good people, this sport has brought into my life. At my first sprint triathlon, I had no idea of the journey I was about to begin and of how triathlon would change my life. That first race was so darn much fun that it whetted my appetite to learn more and to have more triathlon and endurance-sport experiences.

I hope the information, training plans, and encouragement in this book will help you begin a triathlon journey or a fitness journey of your own that will be more fun than you could ever have imagined. I hope your triathlon journey never ends and that endurance sports become an integral part of your life. And I hope your first triathlon race experience is so exhilarating that you can't wait for more. I look forward to seeing you in the pool, on the road, or on the trail.

Gale Bernhardt

Glossary

Aerobic, Aerobic metabolism: Energy production that requires oxygen.

Aerobic capacity: A term used in reference to VO_2max (*see* VO_2max). Aerobic capacity training is in the range of 90 to 100 percent of VO_2max pace, or 95 to 98 percent of maximal heart rate in women (90 to 95 percent in men).

Anaerobic, Anaerobic metabolism: Energy production that does not require oxygen.

Arteries: Blood vessels that conduct blood rich in oxygen away from the heart, to the body.

ATP: Adenosine triphosphate molecules are where potential energy is stored for use at the cellular level.

Brick: A bike ride immediately followed by a run or run/walk.

Circulatory: Usually in reference to blood flow throughout the body.

Combo: A combination workout of two or more sports, one followed immediately by the other. (Except for cycling followed by running, which is typically called a "brick.")

Concentric contraction: A muscle contracts, exerts force, shortens, and overcomes the resistance. For example, concentric contraction occurs in the quadriceps muscles when lifting the weight in a knee extension exercise.

Eccentric contraction: A muscle contracts, exerts force, lengthens, and is overcome by a resistance. For example, eccentric contraction occurs in the quadriceps muscles when lowering the weight in a knee extension exercise.

Economy: When used in reference to exercise, the oxygen consumption required for a given pace. Improving economy means achieving the fastest possible speed at the lowest energy cost.

Extension: Movement about a joint that increases the angle between the bones on either side of the joint.

Fartlek: Swedish term for "speed play." It is characterized by fast-paced exercise bouts that are inserted into a workout at intervals, at the athlete's discretion. Full recovery follows each fast bout.

Flexion: Movement about a joint that brings the bones on either side of the joint closer together.

Isometric contraction: A muscular contraction whereby the muscle exerts force but does not change in length.

Kicking: A swimming term that refers to kicking only, no arms, in the pool. Kicking can be performed while swimming on the back, on either side, or with the belly button pointing toward the bottom of the pool, a prone position. In the prone position, the swimmer can use a kickboard or go without one.

Lactate: Substance formed when lactic acid within the cells enters the bloodstream, and lactate ions separate from hydrogen ions.

Lactate threshold: The point during exercise when increasing intensity causes blood lactate levels to accumulate. It is this accumulation and the associated changes in the body that are thought to cause the burning sensation in working muscles.

Lactic acid: Substance produced within the cell from anaerobic carbohydrate metabolic activity.

Measures:

Metric to English Conversion Factors	English to Metric Conversion Factors
1 kilometer (km) = 0.62 mile (mi.)	1 mi. = 1.61 km
1 meter (m) = 1.09 yards (yd.)	1 yd = 0.914 m
1 centimeter (cm) = 0.3937 inch (in.)	1 in = 2.54 cm
1 millimeter (mm) = 0.039 in.	1 in. = 25.4 mm
1 kilogram (kg) = 2.205 pounds (lb.)	1 lb. = 0.4536 kg
1 liter (l or L) = 0.264 gallon (gal.)	1 gal. = 3.785 L
1 L = 1.057 quarts (qt.)	1 qt. = 0.946 L

Metric Conversions

1 cm = 0.01 m	1 m = 100 cm
1 mm = 0.001 m	1 m = 1,000 mm

Negative-split: A workout or interval in which the second half is executed faster than the first half.

Proprioceptive Neuromuscular Facilitation (PNF): A stretching technique originally developed as a rehabilitative physical therapy procedure. There are several different types of PNF stretching. The one used in this book is the contract–relax technique.

Pull: When used in reference to a swimming workout, a pull buoy is placed between the legs to eliminate any kicking. Only arms are used to propel the swimmer through the water.

Repetitions (reps): In strength training, this refers to the number of times a weight is lifted in a single work bout, without resting. In gym slang, "rep" replaces repetition. For example, fifteen reps of a squat exercise is fifteen repetitions done without resting between repetitions. If rest follows repetitions, beginning to lift again is considered the next set. (*See* Set.)

Rest interval (RI): The amount of rest time following a designated run, bike, or swim. The speed of the swim, bike, or run is not a factor in determining length of RI. The athlete rests for the full time designated. For example, if the swimming workout is ten repeats of 50 yards with a 30-second RI, the athlete takes a full 30 seconds of rest no matter how fast or slow he or she swims. (Different from send-off. *See* Send-off.)

Send-off: When used in reference to a swimming workout, the swimmer pushes off the wall on a set interval. For example, if the send-off is 45 seconds, the swimmer begins a new swim at 45 seconds; 1 minute, 30 seconds; 2 minutes, 15 seconds; 3 minutes; etc. In this case, the speed of the actual swim does not affect the send-off time. In other words, no matter how fast or slow the swim, you leave every 45 seconds. (Different from a rest interval. *See* Rest interval.)

Set: In strength training, the number of times a particular exercise is repeated. Within a single set, the number of repetitions (*see* Repetitions) of the exercise is also designated. For example, three sets of twelve repetitions of a squat exercise means the athlete will complete one set by squatting twelve times. That set is followed by rest. After the rest, the athlete will complete another set, again squatting twelve times. The second set is followed by rest, then by the last set of twelve repetitions.

Transition: In a triathlon, the segment of time between sports. After the swim, heading to the bike is transition number one, often called T1. After the bike ride is finished, the time it takes to dismount the bike, change to running gear, and exit the transition area running is transition number two, often called T2.

Transition area: The area used to store equipment and to change from one sport to another.

Veins: Blood vessels that return blood from the body to the heart.

Ventilation: The circulation of air—in this context, having to do with the lungs. Ventilatory threshold is the rate of exercise, whereby the relationship between ventilation and oxygen consumption deviates from a linear function. Breathing at ventilatory threshold becomes noticeably labored.

VO_2max: A quantitative measure of an individual's ability to transfer energy aerobically. The value is typically expressed in terms of (ml x kg^{-1} x min^{-1}), milliliters of oxygen consumed per kilogram of body weight, per minute. The maximum value can be measured in a laboratory, where resistance is incrementally increased on a bicycle ergometer and the test subject's oxygen consumption is constantly measured. As the workload increases, there is a point when the test subject's oxygen consumption no longer increases to meet the increasing demand of the workload. The maximum oxygen consumption value achieved is considered VO_2max.

Index

seat height, 24–27
seat tube, 21
seat tube angle, 14, 22
send-off, 229
set, 229–30
Shanahan, Don, 2
shoes. *See* running shoes
single-sport athletes, xiv, xv
skin suits, 9
SM. *See* Strength Maintenance
socks, 12, 36
soft pedaling, 170
speed
    bicycle's improvement of, 12
    building, xii, 129
    power output and, 19
speed play, 67
spin-ups, 76–77, 103
sports bars, 68, 91
sports drinks, 67, 78, 91, 104
sprint distance, 4
sprint distance racing
    fit beginner plan, 73–84
    fit beginner team plan, 129–48
    swimming time trial, 56
    unfit beginner plan, 59–72
    unfit beginner team plan, 115–28
stacking, 60–61, 74
static flexibility, 209
stem, 30–32
strength exercises, 187–208
    abdominal curls, 199–200
    correct performance of, 187
    floor back extension, 200–201
    heel raise, 204–5
    hip extensions, 186, 187
    knee extension, 203–4

knee flexion, 201–3
leg press, 190–91
push-up, 196–97
routine, 61
seated cable lat pull-down, 193–94
seated cable, low row, 197–98
squat, 187–88
standing bent-arm lat pull-down, 192–93
standing machine hip abduction, 207–8,
standing machine hip adduction, 205–7
step-up, 189–90
supine dumbbell chest press, 194–95
Strength Maintenance (SM), 185, 186–87
strength training, 183–208
    beginning, 184–85
    equipment for, 187
    minimum exercises, 185
    as part of training plan, 61, 73, 74, 88, 100
    purposes of, 186
    during recovery weeks, 187
    routines, 102
    warm-ups, 184
    when to do, 183–84
stretching, 209–16
    order of exercises, 211
    when to do, 210
stretching exercises
    seated adductor stretch, 214–15
    seated back, hip, and gluteus stretch, 213–14
    standing hamstring stretch, 212

About the Author

Gale Bernhardt is the author of *The Female Cyclist: Gearing up a Level,* *Training Plans for Multisport Athletes,* and *Workouts in a Binder: Swim Workouts for Triathletes* (coauthor). She actively competes and has been instructing athletes since 1974. Bernhardt was selected by USA Triathlon as the men's and women's triathlon coach for the 2004 Olympic Games in Athens, Greece. She was also 2003 coach of the Pan Am Games for the men's and women's teams. She serves and consults on national committees and boards, providing input for triathlon trials and Olympic selection.